THE TWO TONE STORY

By George Marshall

There were six of them, boisterous and laughing, coming down the road towards us. Cocky little skinheads in Harrington jackets and Levi's rolled up over the ankles of their DMs. They were going to see The Specials at The Pavillion. Their leader had a snub nose and bad teeth.

"You goin' to the concert?" he asked Dammers.

"S'pose so", said Dammers, as he turned to walk back with them to Hemel Hempstead.

"Where you from?" they asked him.

"Coventry", Dammers replied.

"You come all this way down from Coventry for the gig then?", they asked, amused.

"Sort of", said Dammers.

"Why?", they asked.

"I'm in the group", he said.

"The Specials?", they asked, excited now.

"S'right", said Dammers.

"Who are you then?", they asked. "'Orace?"

"I'm Jerry", said Dammers.

"Jerry who?" they asked, laughing; a little suspicious.

"I don't remember you on *Top Of The Pops*", said the young skinhead with the snub nose and the bad teeth.

"I was probably hiding", he said.

Allan Jones - *Melody Maker*

This book is dedicated to my Mum, my family and my young lady Rhona.

The Two Tone Story (pbk)

© George Marshall. 1990. 1993.

ISBN No. 0 9518497 3 5

Published by S.T. Publishing, Scotland.
Printed by Pyramid Press, England.

Also by the same author:

Spirit Of '69 - A Skinhead Bible (S.T. Publishing, 1991)
Bad Manners (S.T. Publishing, 1992)
Total Madness (S.T. Publishing, 1993)

All rights reserved. No part of this book may be reproduced in any form by any electronic or mechanical means, including information storage or retrieval systems, without permission in writing from the publisher, except by reviewers who may quote brief passages. So there.

This edition is made available as part of *The Compact Two Tone Story*. Thanks to Steve Davis and Phil Patterson at Chrysalis, Pete Gildon (wherever you are now) and Tanzy at EMI for including this book in an official 2 Tone release. It's a dream come true for me, it really is.

I'd like to thank everyone who has made this book possible, with special thanks going to Jerry Dammers and all who sailed in the good ship 2 Tone for giving me some of the best years of my life. John Bradbury and Neville Staples particularly deserve my gratitude for their help with the book, as do Helen English and Roy Eldridge at Chrysalis for their time and trouble. It just goes to show that the majors can still help the little people. Thanks too go to Alan Sinclair who saved my neck at the last moment. Quotes in this book come from a variety of sources, including a boxful of cuttings I collected over the years. Unfortunately, I did not note where the cuttings came from at the time, but would like to thank *New Musical Express*, *Sounds*, *Melody Maker* and *Smash Hits* for their unintentional help with this book and for contributing so much to yet another misspent youth. Thanks also to Glasgow University Library and Glasgow Mitchell Library, both excellent working environments. Last, but not least I'd like to thank the readers of *Zoot!* who made up the bulk of the buyers of the first edition, and thanks too to Lol Pryor at Dojo and Mark Brennan at Captain Oi! for their support over the years. And finally, I'd like to say hello to anyone who sported a crop and a Specials badge during those dance crazy 2 Tone days. This book's for you.

S.T. PUBLISHING, P.O. Box 12, Dunoon, Argyll. PA23 7BQ. Bonnie Scotland.

THE TWO TONE STORY

Contents

1. A Message To You Rudy — 4
2. Dawning Of A New Era — 7
3. Gangsters — 14
4. Ruder Than You — 32
5. Missing Words — 56
6. Enjoy Yourself — 61
7. It Doesn't Make It Alright — 66
8. In The Studio — 77
9. Ghost Town — 90
10. You're Wondering Now — 94
11. Discography — 97

A MESSAGE TO YOU, RUDY

It's not every day that you fall in love. It's not every day that you would want to. But back in 1979 I was completely bowled over by the sounds coming out of a stylish little number decked out in black and white checks. And I've been having a one way love affair with 2 Tone ever since.

Welcome to my world of 2 Tone. It's my world because that's the way this book has got to be. To me, it's a crime that nobody has felt the need to write a similar book before and so in lots of ways, this is the book that I have always wanted to buy in a bookshop.

To a lot of people, 2 Tone was just another record label that put out good or bad records, depending on your taste. It was nothing more and nothing less. Little pieces of black vinyl that were in fashion one year and out the next.

But to me it was so much more. Almost everything in fact. There was (and is) nothing special about me. I was just one of the countless skinheads, mods, rudies, punks and normals who filled the ranks of the 2 Tone movement. But if 2 Tone was just another record label, I wouldn't be sitting here writing this and you certainly wouldn't be sitting there reading it.

No, 2 Tone represented so much more to so many people. Probably far more than Jerry Dammers and the rest of the crew could ever have hoped for or have even ever realised. For many it was almost a way of life, and remains so to this day. It certainly changed more lives than could possibly ever be calculated. Even with the benefit of hindsight it is impossible to put your finger on it, but there was something very special about the rudest record label of them all.

2 Tone music wasn't just something to listen to. Once you had given those black and white discs a spin on the old dansette, that was it. There was no turning back. The infectious beat got inside you and just wouldn't let go. It became part of you and you became part of it.

Then there were the lyrics. Giving the thoughts of a generation of youngsters a voice that would actually be heard. Hitting out at just the right targets. Turning the world of bubble gum pop upside down and giving it a good kick up the arse into the bargain. Al Capone's guns still didn't argue.

Next up was the style. Smart suits, Ben Sherman's, sta prest and loafers, mingling with Fred Perry's, bleached Levi's and boots n' braces. Pork pie hats, sheepies, Harringtons, crombies and flight jackets - all of them got an airing. And of course black and white was everywhere as 2 Tone swept the nation. Even the Union Jack was almost temporarily replaced by a chequered flag.

But the most important part of 2 Tone was the youngsters on the streets, wearing the clothes, playing the tunes and living their lives. They were the ones who gave 2 Tone a place in their hearts and took it to the very top. Heady days they were too and some great times were had, but more than anything I'll never forget the feeling of belonging. Belonging to something that was really important, that really meant something, that people really took notice of. And most importantly something that was really a part of you. For me, the kid on the corner of the street sporting a Specials badge was just as important as The Specials themselves.

All of the above contributed to an atmosphere that was unique to those 2 Tone days. The ivory tower brigade can knock it all they like, but there's no disputing that fact. 2 Tone in a nutshell can't be described any better than it was on the sleeve of the album, *This Are Two*

Tone.

"People sometimes ask me whether or not 2 Tone tried to say anything. I always reply that it said a lot. It said LOOK, anyone can do this! It said LISTEN, these are the hopes and fears of a generation reared on Maggie's Farm! But, more than anything, it said DANCE!!!"

Adrian Thrills - *This Are Two Tone*

A generation was raised on some of the sharpest sounds you are likely to hear. And their message was crystal clear.

Don't you know, we're ruder than you!

George Marshall.

Above: Jerry Dammers, founder of The Specials and the 2 Tone label.
(photo courtesy of Chrysalis Records Ltd. All rights reserved)

THE DAWNING OF A NEW ERA

Like a certain national pastime, the music business is a funny old game. Some of the strangest creatures find fame and fortune, while some of the most talented never graduate beyond playing down their local to a handful of punters and a dog. Such is the way of the world I suppose. But you can forget how the story goes, because genuine overnight success in the music business is about as common as a bacon roll at a barmitzvah.

Jerry Dammers, you'll be pleased to hear, might not be one of life's bacon rolls, but I'm sure he'd be the first to agree that he's certainly a strange (and talented) creature. Music journalists have been trying to put their finger on him ever since he first hoisted the Jolly Roger over the 2 Tone camp, but good old Jerry is far too complex a character to be confined to paper by mere words. Jerry Dammers is the legendary mad professor personified. His bumbling exterior, complete with a gormless, toothless smile, was the perfect disguise for the buzzing hive of ideas and activity hiding behind it. A sort of Mr. Magoo with vision. On stage, Dammers was as mad as a hatter, jumping around behind the keyboards like a man possessed. Off stage, he came across as a quiet introvert, who never liked giving interviews. He preferred to let the music do the talking. And as someone once said, "Some people like to blow their own trumpet, but Jerry doesn't even have a trumpet".

Dammers, whose real name is Gerald Dankey, was born in India in 1954, and he lived there with his family for the first two years of his life. Then they moved back to England, first to Sheffield and then on to Coventry. His father was a member of the clergy, and Jerry was brought up in a strict, respectable vicarage. And how he hated it! He hated having to go to church and he hated having to sing in the choir. By the time he'd reached his teens, he started to rebel against everything his family stood for.

"I used to go a bit mad", Dammers once said. "I used to be a mod. A mini-mod. Then I grew my hair longer. When I was 15, I planned to run away from home. I went with a friend to Ireland to some island off the coast. It was a sort of hippy commune. I stuck it for two weeks and then went back home. When I came back, I freaked out completely. I got into this suedehead type of thing. When I was about 17, I got badly into drink and vandalism. I used to get really pissed and put my feet through shop windows and things like that."

His career as a drunken vandal came to an abrupt end one summer when he went on holiday to Torquay with a load of mates. They were walking down the middle of the road and forced an approaching car to stop. But the car with its family of holiday-makers inside, didn't stop quickly enough for our Jerry who climbed on to its roof and started jumping up and down. That was until the roof collapsed. He ended up in court and got off with a hefty £250 fine.

He left school at 16 with one A-Level in Art to his credit and went to art college, first to Nottingham and then to Coventry's Lanchester Polytechnic, where he spent most of his time making cartoon films. Although he got his degree, he never bothered to collect it. Apart from his interest in film-making, Dammers had always wanted to be in a band. Early influences were skinhead reggae from his suedehead days and bands like Slade and The Faces, but it was seeing The Who perform *My Generation* on television that finally made up his mind to be a musician. "It wasn't the flash or the glamour of it. It was just the music. I hate the flash of it. I hate the glamour."

You've heard words like those countless times, usually spoken with all of the sincerity of a Maggie Thatcher blow-up doll, but when they come out of Dammers mouth, you can take them as gospel. While most musicians do anything to get their mug in the 'papers, Jerry would do anything to keep his out.

After leaving school, Jerry played in a lot of bands with great names like Peggy Penguin & The Southside Greeks and The Sissy Stone Soul Band, but with little else but great names to offer the public. For his sins, he ended up doing country & western, rock n' roll, reggae, funky soul, the works. He was also writing a lot of songs at the time (Dammers penned *Little Bitch*, which eventually appeared on The Specials' debut album, when he was 15), but nobody wanted to play them. Those were the days of bubble gum pop and little else, with most little time bands never venturing beyond a set of covers.

Then punk happened. Bands like The Sex Pistols knocked the music business clean off its feet, at least temporarily. These young upstarts could hardly play their instrument ("The Damned can play three chords. The Adverts can play one. Hear all four at...") and there they were taking on the world! Anyone could be in a punk band, and at the time it seemed like everyone was. Punk was just what Dammers had been waiting for.

Dammers became quite a well-known figure on the Coventry punk scene and even then, people had him marked down as something of an eccentric. He also loved reggae and was to be found at just as many blues parties as punk raves. His love of reggae and the energy of punk led him to form his own band. It all started in 1977 with Dammers and Neol Davies, who was later to form The Selecter, making demos on an old Revox in Jerry's front room. Davies and Dammers had met at an audition for a soul band called Night Train. They both joined the band and worked together on and off from then on. Then Jerry went to see a soul band called Breaker which had Horace Panter in its line-up. Horace was in the year above Jerry at Lanchester Poly and they knew each other from there, although not very well. Now he was working as a van driver, quite an asset for any band. After the gig, Dammers asked him if he'd like to help him with the demos he was making, and so one night he went along.

At first Panter wasn't at all sure of what to make of it all, especially since he'd never played reggae before, but he ended up sticking with it. Other musicians came and went from Dammers front room and two songs from those early demo tapes, a primitive version of *Too Much Too Young* and *Jaywalker*, were eventually to appear in later Specials' sets, although the latter never made it past the On Parole Tour of 1978. From these sessions a band emerged called The Automatics. Joining Jerry on keyboards and Horace on bass was one of Jerry's mates Silverton Hutchinson on drums who had also worked with Neol Davies in a band called Chapter 5, and a singer called Tim Strickland, who worked behind the counter at the local Virgin record shop.

Lynval Golding was to join soon afterwards. Lynval was born in Jamaica and moved to England at the age of 13 with his family to live in Gloucester. After leaving school he worked as a car mechanic and then as an engineer. He married at 20 and by the time he teamed up with The Automatics, he had a little girl called Michelle.

"Jerry lived about four doors away from me and I met him at this local called The Pilot," said Lynval. "I already knew Silverton. I'd played in this band with him called Pharaoh's Kingdom, along with Charley Desmond and H from The Selecter. That was when Jerry was with The Sissy Stone Soul Band. Also all of us had played at one time or another with this guy called Ray King who was this sort of Geno Washington-type figure. Jerry's played with him, Neol Davies and H from The Selecter, me. People go and sort of serve their apprenticeship with him."

The Automatics played a handful of gigs with this line-up, playing reggae after a punk fashion, mixing them into a rather clumsy cocktail that went down to varying degrees wherever they set up stall. Their first gig saw Tim singing from scraps of paper because he hadn't learned all the words and Jerry playing the keyboards on the dancefloor, facing the band, because there was no room for him up on the tiny stage. They even got to support Ultravox at a local night club called Tiffany's, which was a real coup for the band at the time.

Poor old Tim didn't last the pace and was soon on his way. A replacement was found in the shape of Terry Hall, who was lead singer with a local new wave punk band called Squad, a band he later described as, "1-2-3-4 then make a noise for two minutes and then stop and say 1-2-3-4 again."

At 18, Terry was the youngest member of the band. He hated school and left as soon as he could, finding work first as a clerk and then as a numistatist (coin and medal dealer in case you were reaching for the dictionary). He enjoyed work about as much as he'd enjoyed his school days, and music and The Squad was his chance to escape from the monotony of life.

Jerry had seen him and thought he was ideal for The Automatics and so the rest of the band agreed to let him join. Terry readily agreed, partly because he was about to be kicked out of Squad who looked like splitting anyway, and partly because he liked their "Stranglers with reggae overtones" sound. Roddy Byers certainly remembers Terry from his Squad days. "He used to be hilarious. They used to support my band. They always used our P.A. and would knack up all the mikes before we went on. Terry used to jump into the audience, spitting at people!"

Nice boy, our Terry.

Dammers had wanted Roddy Byers to join The Automatics when they first formed, but he was too involved with his own band The Wild Boys at the time, a band in the New York Dolls mould which also included future U.K. Subs' drummer, Pete Davies. In fact Roddy wanted Jerry to play with The Wild Boys, but he had just formed The Automatics. Roddy used to go and see them play though, usually at a punk dive called George's where he heard *Too Much Too Young* and *Dawning Of A New Era* for the first time.

Roddy came from a musical family and his father had played the trumpet in a number of soul bands in the Sixties, making quite a name for himself in the Midlands. Punk gave Roddy the opportunity to adopt a new surname, Radiation, which gave him an identity of his own and ended the "Stan Byers' son" label he'd had to live with. Roddy worked as a painter and decorator for the local council which turned out to be a passport to horseplay and the pub.

At a time when The Wild Boys were close to calling it a day, Roddy joined The Automatics almost by accident, after a late night drinking session at another Coventry club, The Domino. "They said they were going down to London the next morning to record some 24 track demos. They wanted me to play guitar on one of the songs. I just said 'Yeeeah!', got drunk and went home. The next morning they were sitting outside my house in a taxi, someone was banging on the door and I was lying in bed thinking, 'Fuck me, they mean it!'."

Roddy had known Jerry quite well from the early punk days, when the Coventry scene was still a close-knit community with everybody knowing everybody else. In fact they had first met way back in 1971, when Jerry auditioned as drummer for a band Roddy was playing bass for. Jerry Dammers didn't get the job. "The worst drummer I've ever heard in my life", commented Roddy.

The Automatics went down to London to record the demos during Easter, 1978, at the expense of Chris Gilbey, who was then manager of Oz punk faves, The Saints. In fact The Automatics made their London debut that Easter Monday, supporting The Saints at The Marquee, but nobody came and the band ended up having to borrow a tenner to get back home. So back to Coventry it was with a few copies of the demo, which were sent on their way in true wannabe fashion to the likes of John Peel.

Then another band called The Automatics stole the Coventry boys' thunder by signing a deal with Island, thereby claiming the name for keeps. A change of name was immediately on the cards and so after trying the likes of The Jaywalkers, The Hybrids and even The Coventry Automatics, they came up with The Special A.K.A. The Automatics. That was a bit of a mouthful and so the name of the band was eventually to be shortened to The Special A.K.A.

When Johnny Rotten left The Pistols, Dammers had this brilliant idea of asking him to join The Automatics, and so off to London he went to find him. Dammers got as far as The Clash's roadie, Roadent, who said he'd pass the tapes on to Rotten to see what he thought. He never did get to see Rotten, but ended up meeting Bernie Rhodes instead who was then manager of The Clash. Jerry told him all about his band and eventually Rhodes agreed to let The Automatics support The Clash on the opening two nights of their forthcoming On Parole Tour (so called because two members of the band had just been prosecuted for various firearms offences, including the shooting of valuable racing pigeons). Dammers wanted The Automatics to play the entire tour and so dragged The Clash's Joe Strummer along to see them. Strummer was an instant convert and told Rhodes that he wanted The Automatics to play the whole tour along with New York punks, Suicide. Rhodes still wasn't convinced, but The Clash had the final say and The Automatics were in business.

Dammers hustling Rotten, Rhodes and Strummer doesn't seem like the shy, quiet introvert he is known as, but his conviction and determination to get what he wants has always shone through. In fact, he quite enjoys the role by some accounts - not that he had much choice because nobody else was up for the job.

The decision to shorten the name to The Special A.K.A. was taken just four hours before the tour's opening night at The Friars in Aylesbury. For The Clash, the tour was to be an overwhelming success, but not so the Coventry lot. Most of the people who were at the gigs had only come to see their heroes, The Clash, and were hardly willing to give the support bands the time of day. Suicide did okay, but The Special A.K.A.'s punky reggae party didn't go down well at all. Terry Hall remembers a typical night at Aberdeen where the band were spat on and had flash cubes and the like thrown at them. What's more, Bernie Rhodes started off by paying them only £25 a night, but when The Clash found out they went mad and made Rhodes double it. Even then, it wasn't really enough to keep the band going.

At least one good thing came from the tour though. Neville Staples was the band's roadie and was always found behind the mixing desk, toasting along to songs. One night before a gig in Leeds, he started singing along to *Monkey Man* as Jerry messed about on the keyboards. From then on, the song was in the set and Neville was in the band.

Neville Staples was a Jamaican who came to the Midlands with his parents when he was 12. He was a real life rude boy outa jail, having been inside a couple of times for theft and housebreaking. Music was now to keep him on the straight and narrow, but once it had put him behind bars when he was caught stealing the wood he needed to build speakers for a sound system.

After the tour, Bernie Rhodes (who Dammers had down as "the most radical member of The Clash") continued to work with the band, but despite what has been written before, he was never officially their manager. "There were a lot of legal things going on," explained Jerry Dammers. "It got as far as a contract being drawn up and there were a lot of arguments about that. Basically, *we* refused to sign *his* contract."

Rhodes took them off to London for six months of disillusionment and little else. Dammers remembers it as being stuck in an empty warehouse with Rhodes turning up now and again with a promoter to see the band run through their set. A bit like a performing circus, but without any of the fun. Rhodes did get them a short residency in Paris, but according to Horace Panter, "It was dreadful, the whole thing, like a Peter Sellers disaster movie."

The bottom line was that the band were hardly being fed, let alone paid, and they began to argue among themselves. Eventually, Silverton had had enough, packed his bags and went home to Coventry. He had a mortgage to pay and so had little choice. It wasn't long before the rest of the band were joining him.

"Rhodes wanted to split us up", remembered Roddy Radiation. "He wanted Terry to join The Black Arabs. He likes to put musicians together like that, but you can't do that with people."

Above: The Specials live!
(Photo courtesy of Chrysalis Records Ltd. All rights reserved)

Back in Coventry, the band came very close to calling it a day. Only the determination of Jerry Dammers kept it together and saw it through a difficult winter period. Most of the the band didn't think they'd get anywhere, but it was obvious Dammers did and since they were all on the dole and had nothing better to do, they stayed with it. Back to Horace. "I think we'd all agree that Jerry got the original set off the ground. He put the band together and originally we were doing his songs. He organised everything. And if there was a final say, it was usually Jerry who had it."

They began to rehearse in the back room of a pub, with Horace bringing in wood for the fire, Jerry playing his keyboards with fingerless gloves and the rest of them refusing to take their coats and jackets off. To make matters worse, Silverton kept missing the practices.

However, Silverton's regular disappearing act turned out to be a blessing in disguise. The band had realised that their brand of punk reggae wasn't working. Rhodes had told them that their sound was too confused, a feeling obviously shared by audiences who didn't know whether to pogo or dance.

"We had songs where part of the songs were reggae, then they'd go into a rock section, then perhaps into reggae", said Jerry. "And it would throw people off. So we sat down and looked at the whole thing and put a definite beat in it all the way through, sort of blended it together."

And anyway, bands like The Ruts, The Members, and even The Clash, were able to produce a far better punk reggae marriage than The Special A.K.A. were managing. Dammers had been wanting to experiment with a music called ska for sometime, as had Lynval Golding. Ska was a Jamaican derivative of R&B and was the grandfather of reggae. It had been tried in the warehouse in London, but Silverton wasn't having any of it. Now with him A.W.O.L., the band were free to experiment with ska again and a slightly different, but better sound began to fall into place. Eventually, Silverton Hutchinson was sacked and the band continued along their new path.

This change in style nearly saw Roddy leave too. He had been with the band about a year and was now being asked to re-think his guitar playing to fit the new sound, a sound he didn't particularly like anyway at the time. "I never really played ska anyway. I was actually playing Chuck Berry rock n' roll things over ska rhythms."

The Special A.K.A. had learned another valuable lesson from Bernie Rhodes, this time about image. Rhodes was a great believer in selling a package, not just the music, and it has paid dividends for a lot of bands he has worked with. The Clash, Dexy's Midnight Runners, Jo Boxers. Whether people like it or not (and musicians generally don't), songs are quickly swallowed up by the music business and churned back out as products to sell to an ever-fickle Joe Public. And image, the way a band looks and acts, is an important part of the package deal. Dammers knew that the band needed an image to bridge the gap between what they were trying to achieve and audience appreciation. What's more, he wanted to create a movement just like punk had. The Sex Pistols would probably have made it on their own, but Dammers believed that they appeared all the more important for being at the head of the punk movement, with countless other bands following in their wake.

Any band playing reggae and ska covers had to look to the style and image of the West Indian rude boy and the British skinhead for inspiration. Pork pie hats, tonic and mohair suits, Ben Sherman and Fred Perry shirts, loafers, brogues, crombies, Harringtons, boots and braces;

all were adopted by the new look Special A.K.A. It was this attention to detail that Dammers hoped would lead to the band being accepted and would lead them on to bigger and better things. This really was to be the dawning of a new era.

Disillusioned by the attitude of the music business, Jerry also wanted to start a record label so that the band could release a debut single. He even had a name for it - 2 Tone Records. Named after the two tone tonic suits worn by mods and skinheads a decade or so ago. It also captured the multi-racial nature of the band, which saw black and white musicians on the same stage playing together at a time when The National Front and The British Movement were becoming as big as they were ever going to be. Dammers had sketch pads full of the designs he wanted to use on the record sleeve. Black and white checks from the pop art days of the Sixties, and a black and white camera negative-type picture of a rude boy, based on a photo of Peter Tosh from one of the Wailing Wailers' early albums. Walt Jabsco, as the rude boy became known, and the black and white checks were to become the trademark of 2 Tone and the British ska movement it was to give birth to.

GANGSTERS

Christmas came and went in time-honoured fashion and by March 1979, The Special A.K.A. and 2 Tone were ready to face an unsuspecting public with their debut single. It was called *Gangsters* and was a re-working of the 1964 Prince Buster ska classic, *Al Capone* (in fact the screeching of brakes at the start of the record was sampled directly from it). *Gangsters* served as a timely and scathing attack on the music industry and in particular the band's treatment at the hands of Bernie Rhodes, who is name-checked and who replaces the Chicago gangster as the song's anti-hero.

"I never understood the lyrics although I wrote them", Jerry once said in typical Dammerspeak fashion. "But, I know it was about the sharks and wide boys that try and make money by pretending to run the music business."

With £700 from a local Coventry businessman and other odds and ends from family and friends, the band was ready to go into the studio. Almost. The only thing missing was a drummer. Finding a replacement for Hutchinson was not as hard as it might have been, because Jerry shared a flat with a bloke called John Bradbury who just happened to be a dab hand with the sticks. Born of Irish parents, Brad had grown up in a world of mod and northern soul. "I remember when I was living in Hull in the mid-70s, I came across this scooter club that had over 200 members and had been going since 1966. The northern soul thing is something that's totally ignored by the media, yet it was so important to kids in the north."

Like Jerry and Horace, Brad has a degree in Fine Art ("I studied art history, but couldn't hold a conversation in it if I tried"), but he attended Hull Poly not Lanchester. While he was supposedly studying, he'd be more often than not drumming in some working men's club with a local soul band. He also had a decent reggae collection, courtesy of his days working at the same Virgin record shop as The Automatics' first singer. "It's funny the way you get burnt at first when buying reggae. At least 75% of the stuff I used to buy is really useless."

And never a truer word was spoken.

Initially, Brad was just called in to play drums on *Gangsters*, but that line-up of Terry Hall and Neville Staples on vocals, Jerry Dammers on keyboards, Sir Horace Gentleman Panter on bass, Lynval Golding and Roddy 'Radiation' Byers on guitars, and John 'J.B.' Bradbury on drums, was to carry The Specials right through to 1981 and their split so soon after the success of *Ghost Town*.

Still, the arrival of Brad didn't solve all of their problems. They only had enough money to record the one track and so either had to find more money or ask another band to play on the flip side. As it went, Neol Davies was offered the chance to be on the single. Incestuous as the music business is, Neol had written an instrumental with John Bradbury back in '77 called *The Selecter* and had recorded it on his old two track Revox. It was decided that this would go out with *Gangsters*. Roger Lomas was called in to engineer the remix and Brad's brother-in-law, a local session musician called Barry Jones, played trombone. They were billed as The Selecter, even though no such band existed at the time.

Jerry Dammers approached Rough Trade to distribute the single. They were one of the biggest names on the indie music scene at the time, and after hearing the tracks, agreed to handle it. A manufacturing and distribution deal was struck and 5,000 copies of the record were pressed, with the band rubber-stamping the plain paper sleeves themselves. Originally, Jerry had only wanted 2,500 pressed, but Rough Trade insisted on double that amount. And not only did 2 Tone's first release feature two bands, but it also had a different catalogue number for each side to underline the fact. *Gangsters* went out as TT1, *The Selecter* as TT2.

To sell 5,000 copies, Dammers knew he needed help and Alan Harrison, a former lecturer at Lanchester, pointed him in the right direction. Harrison had shared a house with a publicist called Rick Rogers for a couple of years and had even tried to interest him in the band when it was still called The Automatics. It wasn't long before Dammers was back in London and knocking on the door of Rogers' Camden Town Office. At the time, Rogers' company Trigger had Chiswick as its main account and Rogers himself was working closely with The Damned, who were then signed to the label.

Rogers listened to the tapes, liked what he heard and that weekend travelled up to Coventry to see The Special A.K.A. play live. "I thought they were the most exciting band I'd seen in ages," said Rick Rogers. "And basically, our relationship grew from there.

"To begin with I didn't think Jerry had much going for himself. He still had his false teeth at the time. And whenever he talked to you, he'd be dribbling down the side of his mouth. It was quite difficult to talk to him and look him straight in the face at the same time. He used to stay at my place whenever they were in London, and gradually I got to know him. He used to talk about his plans, his ideas for 2 Tone. And I began to realise that he was really the heavy king-pin of the whole operation.

"The first thing he wanted was a definite sound, a definite identity for 2 Tone, a definite sound that would be identified with the label. He wanted 2 Tone to become the British equivalent of Stax or Tamla. He was still finding his way about the business, but that's what he was aiming for."

Gangsters achieved cult status within days of its release, thanks to rave reviews in the music press and night time Radio 1 airplay from the man with his finger on the nation's musical pulse, John Peel. To support the release, the band started playing every gig they could get. As well as dates around the country, Rogers got The Special A.K.A. a series of dates in London, headlining smaller venues and picking up some decent support slots in the larger ones. Those were the days when it would only cost a quid or less to see a decent band and no more than three for the biggies. At the time the band's set consisted mainly of the songs that were to appear on their debut album and live EP, although as the bootleg tapes that survive from those early days bear testimony, a few of them still needed a bit of work done on them. That didn't matter though. What counted was the excitement, energy and atmosphere created by one of the best live bands this country has ever seen.

One of the most important of those early gigs was on the 8th of April at The Lyceum, where the band (billed as The Specials) opened up for The U.K. Subs and The Damned. The Subs had a healthy skinhead following who really took to the punk-injected brand of ska being touted by Coventry's finest, and who from then on in, turned up at Specials' gigs in growing numbers. By the time they were supporting the Gang Of Four and The Mekons at The Lyceum at the end of May, the first pressing of *Gangsters* had all but sold out, they'd had front covers and spreads in the music 'papers, and every label in town was vying for the band's signatures. The Special A.K.A. were creating the biggest buzz since The Sex Pistols and there was something in the air telling you that these boys were going to be bloody massive.

Left: The ad that celebrated The Specials signing to Chrysalis and heralded their first British tour. Above: The two ads for the Nashville dates.

It was one of those things that just sucks you in like a huge magnet and you just cannot help but get caught up in it all. Not if you have an ounce of sense anyway.

On the 29th of May, John Peel broadcast The Specials' first Radio 1 session. It featured *Gangsters*, *Too Much Too Young* (a number loosely based on Lloyd Terrell's old Pama fave, *Birth Control*), Roddy Radiation's *Concrete Jungle,* and a straight cover of The Maytals' *Monkey Man*. Brad didn't play on the sessions and so some rather amusing percussion appeared in place of the drums, with Neville Staples taking all the credit for it. As part of The Peel Sessions series, the Strange Fruit label released all four tracks on vinyl in 1987.

This further stamp of approval from John Peel only added to the circus of record company suits that turned up at every gig, along with the likes of new wave fave Elvis Costello, who was an early convert to the 2 Tone sound. A&M, Arista, Island, CBS, Virgin, Warner Bros. They were all sniffing around, offering larger and larger amounts of money to get the hottest property on the market at the time. Christ! Mick Jagger was turning up in person to represent Rolling Stone Records! The band couldn't believe it was all happening to them, but rather than get carried away with it all, they knew exactly what they wanted out of any deal. A distribution deal for their 2 Tone label, giving them the freedom to record what they wanted and to sign other groups of their choice.

At the end of the day, it was Chrysalis who finally got The Special A.K.A. to put pen to paper by agreeing to their demands. Roy Eldridge, a man who had worked on the music 'papers before moving to the A&R department at Chrysalis via the press office, was responsible for signing them.

"It was the best gig I'd ever seen", said Roy remembering the first time he'd ever seen The Specials at the Moonlight Club in Hampstead. "They played upbeat ska with intense lyrics and the band was full of contradictions. Terry Hall was Mr. Dead Pan and Lynval and Neville were going crazy."

The gig was full of A&R men and journalists, and when Eldridge went back stage, Rick Rogers warily agreed to a meeting. The stumbling block with other labels had been 2 Tone. Everyone wanted The Specials, but nobody wanted the label. At Chrysalis too, there were some arguments over creating a seperate label identity, but in the end it was agreed to do just that because the band were too good to lose.

The 2 Tone idea might have put the others off, but the extra money involved turned out to be peanuts. 2 Tone was allowed to record ten singles a year by any band and Chrysalis were obliged to release at least six of them. The budget for each single was only £1,000, and so it was just like giving The Specials another ten grand advance with the added bonus of the chance to discover new talent and more chart success. For that, The Specials signed a five album deal, with options up to eight LPs. With most bands doing well if they are still in business after the "difficult second album", Chrysalis were certainly taking no chances about losing their new signings half way along the road to Beatledom.

2 Tone was never a seperate entity from Chrysalis, although those directly in control decided what was released on it. In effect it was just a trading name for Chrysalis. There were no fancy 2 Tone contracts and bands on 2 Tone were actually signed to Chrysalis. For this, Chrysalis paid 2 Tone a two per cent royalty on top of that offered to the bands. 2 Tone might have been a revolutionary challenge to what had gone before, but when all was said and done Chrysalis still held all of the aces.

Gangsters was back in the shops in black and white paper sleeves, featuring the now legendary black and white checks and Walt Jabsco, the 2 Tone man who was to launch thousands of rude boy immitators. To celebrate the deal and the renewed interest in the single, The Specials set off on a two month tour of the British club circuit. The problem was that some of the clubs were getting too small for the band's growing number of fans. Typical was the gig at London's Nashville on the 8th of June, where so many people wanted to get in that hundreds were turned away and the police had to be called to prevent a near riot outside. The next time they played The Nashville, less than three weeks later, the gig had to be made an all-ticket affair.

Supporting The Specials at both Nashville dates was a North London band by the name of Madness, a six piece outfit who had been doing the rounds in various shapes and guises since 1977.

Life began for Madness when four mates decided to form a band. Introducing Mike 'Barso' Barson on keyboards, Lee 'Kix' Thompson on stolen saxaphone, Chris 'Chrissy Boy' Foreman on guitar and John 'Billy Whizz' Hasler on drums. The fact that they could hardly play their instruments was neither here nor there. It was difficult enough keeping the band together without having to worry about life's little technicalities.

It was June 1977 before the band, then called The North London Invaders, faced the public for the first time at a 'gig' organised by a skinhead friend of theirs, Simon Birdsall. Si was having a party and said the band could play at it. The big day came, and while the party continued indoors, The Invaders were left to knock out a handful of old rock n' roll chestnuts in the back garden. Not the most illustrious of debuts, but they went down well enough in front of those who had bothered to leave the party to watch them. Certainly a skinhead called Carl 'Chas' Smythe was impressed enough to join on bass, and another bloke, Graham 'Suggs' McPherson asked to audition as vocalist.

Suggs went along to the next rehearsal, belted out a dodgy version of *See You Later Alligator* (the only song he knew most of the words to), and he was in. A right motley crew it was too. As with The Specials and Jerry Dammers, the driving force behind The Invaders was the keyboard player, Barso, and from time to time the lack of musical ability and commitment in the band would get to him. He was always getting at Lee for his sax playing and every time he did so, Lee would disappear for a week or more. Chas got the elbow for his appalling bass playing. Hasler's drumming was showing no sign of improving. And Suggs was sacked for going to football once too often when he should have been at band practice.

Things started to look up (they couldn't have got much worse) when Hasler turned up at a rehearsal with a friend, Gary Dovey. The idea was that Hasler would try his hand at singing (on paper not such a bad idea since he did write most of the songs at the time, but when he opened his mouth...) and Dovey would sit in on drums. And as luck would have it, Dovey knew someone who could really play bass, Mark 'Bedders' Bedford, who quickly replaced a certain Gavin Rogers who had stepped into Chas' shoes. With Lee back in the fold (sometimes anyway - even a young lady by the name of Lucinder Garland had stood in for him at a gig in February 1978) it was all starting to come together. That was until Lee decided to clock Dovey one at a rehearsal because of "musical differences", leading to Dovey walking out and quitting the band.

It was getting more like *Soap* every day. The search was on for a new drummer and Bedders brought along Dan 'Woody' Woodgate, who he had played with in a heavy metal band called Steel Erection, to fill the post. Hasler just wasn't up to fronting the band and when Suggs asked to return he was welcomed with open arms. Hasler took the job of manager and had the task of getting the band gigs.

By the end of 1978, The Invaders were finally getting their act together, playing a mixture of originals and covers based loosely on the sounds of Jamaican ska. A nutty sound, according to Lee. "It's 'cos our music sounds like fairgrounds and organs and things. It just sounds nutty", as Chrissy Boy once put it.

The nutty sound was as apt a description as you could get. There was no question about it that these boys were after a good time at night after a day of gardening, plastering, sorting mail, liberating things from shops and being on the dole. They were a good time dance band which was quite an oddity in '78, but their nutty sound, mad antics, clowning around and general Tom Foolery hid a largely forgotten serious side (in later life they seemed to be on *Tiswas* more often than Chris Tarrant, only to eventually get themselves and Stiff's entire rota banned over a custard pie incident). Their lyrics weren't throwaway one-liners, but reflected ordinary everyday life with remarkable accuracy and a touch of humour. *Razor Blade Alley* for example was as cutting as any Stanley knife could be, as was *My Girl*.

Whenever they played, their numbers were boosted by Chas, his brother Brendan, Si, and another skinhead, Andrew 'Chalky' Chalk, and they would dance around on stage while the band played. It might seem a little odd to include friends in a band history, but that's what Madness were all about. A bunch of lads in a band for the crack and to play the music they liked best. And anyway, Chas' role of introducing Madness, his fancy footwork and random shouts, were eventually to find him a permanent place in the band at the end of 1979.

The North London Invaders as a name didn't quite fit the band's all the fun of the fair attitude and so on a spur of the moment suggestion by Chrissy Boy, the band was renamed Madness. The name was taken from the title of the Prince Buster song which was in the set and ended up being the only name they could agree on. So Madness it was. Sheer madness!

As fate would have it, Suggs caught up with The Special A.K.A. by accident, at a Rock Against Racism gig at London's Hope & Anchor. He was amazed to find a band from Coventry playing more or less the same type of music as his own band. Before the gig, he'd never even heard of The Special A.K.A., or 2 Tone for that matter. He got talking to Jerry Dammers after the show, they swapped addresses and it wasn't long before Jerry was introduced to the rest of the band. He asked them to support The Special A.K.A. at the Nashville and they jumped at the chance. The only problem was that the Nashville date clashed with Madness' first ever date at Camden Town's Dublin Castle, a gig they'd been after for ages and only secured because they said they were a jazz band. This little problem was solved in true Madness style. They played both gigs. And just about got away with it by the skin of their teeth.

Now that 2 Tone was up and running under the watchful eye of Chrysalis, Barso knocked together a rough press release and sent it in. Dammers had liked Madness and it wasn't long before he asked them to record a single for the label. As it happened, Madness had just recorded a three track demo at London's tiny Highbury Studios with ex-Deaf School man, Clive Langer, who now worked as a solo act and a producer. And two of those tracks were to find their way on to the band's debut single. *The Prince* was the nutty boys' tribute to the King of Ska, Prince Buster, who had supplied the band with the B side, *Madness*. The third track, a version of *My Girl* with Mike Barsons doing the honours on vocals, didn't go to waste however, and later appeared on the 12" of *The Return Of The Los Palmas 7* (Stiff).

The early days of Madness were captured in the brilliant film, *Take It Or Leave It*, now available as a Virgin video. Definitely one worth adding to your collection.

After the second Nashville gig, The Specials continued on their tour of British clubs before arriving back in the Big Smoke for the re-opening of the newly sound-proofed Electric Ballroom on July 21st. It was to be a special 2 Tone Evening and the bill for the night was The Specials, Madness and the newly formed The Selecter (Dexy's Midnight Runners were also advertised, but didn't play in the end). The place was mobbed, with crowds of skins, mods, punks and a few normals almost blocking Camden High Road in their bid to get in. Once inside, everyone was drawn on to the floor by a night of dance music in its purest form. The Selecter, appearing live for the first time, went down well and were followed by those London wide boys, Madness, who went down a storm on their home turf. Then The Specials took the place to near boiling point with soon to be classic after classic. And to round the night off in what was to become true 2 Tone fashion, The Specials were joined on the heaving stage by Madness, The Selecter and half the audience for an encore of the old Pioneers' classic, *Long Shot Kick De Bucket*. Anyone who was privileged enough to be there must have sensed that they were witnessing the start of something big. Something very big. And if they'd linked the Electric Ballroom up to the national grid that night, it would have lit up half of North London no problem.

Above: It's Madness!
(Photo courtesy of Chrysalis Records Ltd. All rights reserved)

As July came to an end, *Gangsters* found its way into the Top Thirty. Now, the charts aren't usually the be all and end all of good music, but on this occassion The Special A.K.A. found themselves rubbing shoulders with the likes of The Boomtown Rats, The Sex Pistols,

The Buzzcocks, The Police, The Ruts and Sham 69. Oh, and Abba and Cliff were in there too so as not to let the side down. Over the coming weeks *Gangsters* made its way up the charts and by the end of August had reached the dizzy heights of number six (it would certainly have gone higher if it hadn't sold 50,000 copies before receiving any day-time radio play).

A week after *Gangsters* became eligible for Top Of The Pops, Madness made their vinyl debut with *The Prince* (2 Tone CHS TT3). If *Gangsters* had secured the beaches, *The Prince* heralded the oncoming 2 Tone invasion. And if you weren't in the mood for dancing, you had to find yourself a seat. Despite rave reviews in the music press and the 2 Tone seal of approval, the record made a surprisingly slow start in the chart stakes, but eventually reached number 16 in early October and stayed in the charts for 11 weeks. Meantime, Madness had had their first Radio 1 Session thanks again to John Peel, which featured a different version of *The Prince*, *Bed & Breakfast Man*, *Land Of Hope & Glory* and *Stepping Into Line* (given the Strange Fruit treatment and released in 1986). They also took to the road, with the pick of the gigs being a support slot with The Pretenders and the August bank holiday weekend bash down at The Lyceum, featuring The Selecter as well as mod faves Secret Affair, The Purple Hearts and Little Rooster. The next day most of the mods and skins in the audience were off down to Southend to bathe in the sun and to do battle with the teds and rockers. Seaside battles were back in fashion.

Success is all about being in the right place at the right time. And if you're hoping to put your finger on the reason for 2 Tone's success, I don't think that's too far off the mark. When bands like The Specials and Madness entered the musical arena, it was already playing host to the 1978 return of the skinheads and to the 1979 march of the mods. Talk about landing on your feet. It was the mods who'd first warmed to the sound of ska, or blue beat as it was known then, and it was the skinheads who were championing Jamaican music as the swinging decade came to an end. So it's little wonder that both cults provided a massive injection of recruits into the 2 Tone army come '79. *Gangsters* was released the same week that *Quadrophenia* had its premiere, and although The Special A.K.A. initially found themselves on punk and new wave bills, it wasn't long before mod and ska bands were playing together.

Besides its skinhead and mod following, 2 Tone also gave birth to the rude boy cult. There had been rude boys back in the Sixties, but they were mainly blacks of West Indian origin. By 1979 and 2 Tone, the rude boys had all the trappings of a good old British youth cult. Taking their style from their mod and skin brethren, and their name from the young rowdies of downtown Jamaica who had been both glorified and chastised by Jamaican ska and rocksteady records a decade and more before, rude boys and rude girls had no other musical allegiance other than to ska. There was often little difference between the appearance of a rude boy and a skinhead or a mod, particularly at the younger end of the scale where your commitment and knowledge was usually measured by the number of button badges you had. Quite often you'd see a kid strolling along with a crew cut, Fred Perry, Harrington, jeans and loafers and he could have been any one of the three. It's all a labels game anyway and the kids, although proud to belong to their particular cult, were more interested in the music.

One thing the rudies did like though was anything in the colours black and white. There was no prettier sight than watching the checked mini-skirts walking by. I remember once having to explain to a school friend's distressed mum what exactly her daughter had meant when she'd announced that she was a rude girl. The name certainly raised a few eyebrows anyway.

The media attention being focused on 2 Tone further added to its meteoric rise to the top of the music pile. The music 'papers were in there, the tabloids, the television, the radio, all feeding the fire that was engulfing a nation's youth. It seemed like every kid in town was off

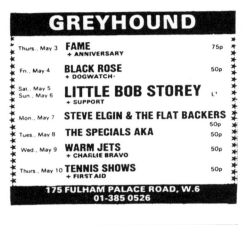

More gig ads from the early days of 2 Tone, including The Specials bottom of the bill or tucked away with also ran bands. And they couldn't even spell The Selecter correctly in the ads!

down the barber's for a crew cut, and black sta-press trousers and white socks meant the old school uniform would never be quite the same again.

Even at this early stage, the best made plans were knocked for six by what was quickly becoming a runaway train. Not even the most optimistic member of the 2 Tone camp could have forecast such rapid success for the label and almost from day one it was like the proverbial Frankenstein monster that nobody could really control. It was all Dammers and Co. could do to keep the train on the rails, let alone decide what direction it would take. The Specials' second single and one from The Selecter had been pencilled in for September, but the pressure of events meant that neither saw the light of day until the following month. The Specials, The Selecter and Madness were all busy gigging in Britain and in The Specials case Europe too, and there just wasn't the time to play the studio game.

Madness were only committed to the one single with 2 Tone and as *The Prince* found its way into the charts, the record company executives made their way to the band's gigs, all looking for the next big thing because of all the talk about a "ska revival". Elton John's Rocket label and Virgin sidekick, Dindisc, were in particularly hot pursuit, with numerous other labels following in their trail.

"The old record labels have no insight", said Suggs at the time, "And the only reason half of them go after a band is because someone else is going after them. If someone's interested in you, they're all interested in you. Island didn't even know we had *The Prince* out when it was at 73. They'd just heard that everyone else was interested in us."

At the start of October the chase was over. Madness signed to Stiff Records after playing at Stiff boss Dave Robinson's wedding. "They came to take the piss", he said, "But I thought they were wonderful. They even got Elvis Costello to dance, which is a thing you don't do too often. They literally dragged him on to the floor!"

There was no ill-feeling between Madness and The Specials and 2 Tone. Quite the opposite in fact. At the time, the 2 Tone deal for bands besides The Specials only went as far as single releases and did not cover albums. If Madness wanted to release an album, which they did, it would have involved negotiating a new contract, and at 2 Tone there was always the danger that Madness would end up playing in the shadow of The Specials anyway. For their part, Chrysalis were obviously interested in signing Madness, but at the end of the day they weren't too disappointed to lose them. Chrysalis had quite enough on their plate dealing with The Specials. So Stiff it was, with Sire picking up the band for the USA.

October was to be a busy month for 2 Tone too. In June, Neol Davies had put a band to the The Selecter name. Their first vinyl offering was *On My Radio* backed by *Too Much Pressure* (both penned by Davies), which was released in early October (2 Tone CHS TT4). *On My Radio* was a straight forward attack on the music policy of radio stations, and in particular Radio 1, who play safe, bland pop virtually all day long. It made every playlist in the country and quickly followed Madness into the charts, making it to number eight (a year later a flexidisc re-mix of the track was given away free with the first issue of *Flexipop* magazine).

The Specials were also on their way back to the charts with *A Message To You Rudy* (2 Tone CHS TT5), a faithful version of the Dandy Livingstone classic, which just scraped into the Top Ten. "A bit of Jamaican wisdom and one of the first ska tunes The Specials ever played", said Dammers. "Ska was much more fun for a band to play than rock, and a bit more fun for the audience who had to listen to it."

A Message To You Rudy saw The Specials' line-up expand with the introduction of Dick Cuthell on cornet and a Jamaican legend, Rico Rodriguez on trombone. Born in 1934, Rico had learned his trade at the famous Alpha Boys' Catholic School with Don Drummond of The Skatalites fame as his tutor, a role often adopted by older pupils. Alpha has had a long tradition of producing some of JA's top musicians and in particular horn men.

"Drummond was a quiet person, but a very strict teacher. We were friends, but when it came to teaching, it was very serious. If Drummond didn't teach me well, and the bandmaster came along to check you, and you were not good, that reflected on the teacher."

Rico's first recording session was in 1958, on Theophilius Beckford's *Easy Snappin'* for Clement Dodd (regarding by many as one of the first songs to hint at a move from R&B to the birth of ska). Before leaving for England in 1961, Rico also worked for Duke Reid and Prince Buster, who along with Dodd were the top dogs on the Jamaican music scene at the time. As such, Rico's trombone playing appears on songs by the likes of Laurel Aitken, Derrick Harriot, Jackie Edwards and countless other Jamaican stars. Over in England, he continued to do session work and solo work, but to make ends meet he worked at the local gas works, then on the production line in a car factory and even as a painter for the local council. He released albums in his own right on both Trojan and Pama, but his big break came when to signed to Island for the release of the album, *Man From Wareika*, in 1977. It was critically acclaimed and enabled him to start touring again. In 1979, he was appearing at London clubs playing ska, reggae, blues and rasta with his own backing band, which included his long-time friend and colleague, Dick Cuthell. He was no stranger to modern music, having guested with The Members on *Offshore Banking Business* (Virgin), and when he returned from a visit to Jamaica to hear that The Specials were trying to get hold of him, the man went straight for the 'phone.

Rico not only gave The Specials a direct link with Jamaican ska (he actually played on the original, *Rudy A Message To You*), but he also gave them the respectability in those circles that wrote 2 Tone off as second rate plunderers of a glorious past. The truth was that The Specials, Madness and the others were so much more than ska revivalists. They injected that infectious ska beat with the freshness and reality of life in 1979 Britain, bringing it bang up to date without taking the piss.

"Some writers and men like this y'know, they say that The Specials is stealing reggae and ska from the black man," commented Rico. "But this is just pure foolishness, just pure fuckery, these things they say. For when I lived in Jamaica I played sometimes as part of The Skatalites. And even before The Skatalites were playing together, I was playing this music and was a most loved and respected musician in Jamaica. So would I be playing with The Specials if the things these people say are true?"

Rico wasn't the only member of the old ska guard who had nothing but praise for The Specials and 2 Tone. The singer, Laurel Aitken, widely acknowledged as the man who brought ska to these shores and known as the Godfather Of Ska, had the following to say on the subject.

"Lots of people said that they were ripping off the original sound of ska, but I wouldn't say that because lots of black people don't want to play ska. So it was great for me to see Jerry Dammers and his posse doing what they were doing because a lot of black people weren't interested in it. I don't know why. You see they want to play reggae. Reggae and ska are the same thing - except it's just a change of drum beat or a different drop of the bass."

On the flip side of *A Message To You Rudy* was the punky ska of *Nite Klub*, which featured Chrissie Hynde from The Pretenders on backing vocals. A line from the song, "I won't

dance in a club like this, all the girls are sluts and the beer tastes just like piss", summed up the trendy club scene then as it does now. At the time, a lot of clubs had a "No Skinheads" door policy and so this was The Specials' two-fingered salute to such dives. In fact a couple of months before the release of this single, The Specials and The Selecter had organised a boycott of Barbarellas night club in Birmingham, after the management refused entry to anyone who vaguely resembled a skinhead to a gig. The bands only went on stage after the owner said that they wouldn't get paid and no refunds would be given to their fans.

Both *A Message To You Rudy* and *Nite Klub* found their way on to The Specials' official debut album, *Specials* (2 Tone CDL TT 5001), which was released during the last week of October, as was Madness' debut LP, *One Step Beyond* (Stiff). Official because a bootleg album of The Specials live in Manchester had been released that summer. *Specials* featured 14 tracks taken from the band's live set and captured in TW Studios by producer, Elvis Costello. It perfectly captured the punk-ska marriage that was The Specials. Ska with balls to coin a phrase. The sentiment and noise of punk was thrown into a Molotov cocktail of highly infectious ska and all you needed was a record player to light the spark.

Other highlights of the album were the Dammers' penned *Blank Expression* and Roddy Radiation's *Concrete Jungle*, along with *Too Much Too Young* and the cover of *Monkey Man*. In fact there's not a weak track on it and everyone will have their own favourites. *Gangsters* was not on the vinyl version of the album (except in the States), but found its way on to the end of its cassette sister.

The album got a surprisingly mixed reception in the music press, with Elvis Costello taking most of the flak. The critics were quick to pick up on a feeling that the band were resting too heavily on the praise heaped on *Gangsters* and live performances. Terry Hall's vocals could also have been mixed better, and the feeling was that the album as a whole tended to lack any real rhythm - something that the band were not happy about either.

"I don't think Elvis quite understood what we were aiming for", said Roddy Byers. "I think he still thought it was like one section of reggae, then the next section's a heavy section, then another section comes along. But I'm not knocking him at all. He's got a great drum sound and he was a lot better than having some hot-shot producer who wouldn't even let us in to the mixing sessions."

Dammers didn't know what all the fuss was about. And neither did the buying public who voted with their money and put *Specials* straight into the top five and kept it in the charts for 45 weeks. "Elvis Costello was just someone who liked us and wanted to do the album. He just came to all our bookings. No one else did. He said he liked us and wanted to produce us. We all got on with him, and he got on with the job."

Too many music journalists try to read far too much into bands and their music and end up adding two and two together to get 793. A bit like how English teachers hang on every word that poor old Shakespeare ever wrote. The classic hurdle that saw many a good journalist fall was mistaking lyrics written from a personal point of view for sexism. There was quite a little debate about it all and it cropped up in record and gig reviews galore, while The Specials got on with living in the real world. They made socially aware, riotous dance music and you could take it or leave it. And if the music 'papers couldn't see that through their guest passes and assorted freebies, at least the kids on the street could.

After taking over the nation's airwaves, a massive 40 date tour of the British Isles under a 2 Tone Tour banner was arranged. Although now signed to Stiff, Madness agreed to join The

Specials and The Selecter for the first half of the invasion of Britain's towns and cities. All three bands spent a week rehearsing at the Roundhouse in London before kicking off the tour at Brighton's Top Rank on October the 19th.

Brighton was to start in true rock n'roll fashion with the coach that was carrying all three bands arriving a few hours later than planned. As a result both The Selecter and Madness had only rushed sound checks and their sound on the night suffered consequently. Not that the packed Top Rank cared as its occupants danced away. The Selecter were the perfect warm up, Madness had some of the crowd on the stage for a couple of numbers and The Specials seemed to have them up there for the entire set.

And that was the pattern for the rest of the tour. The 2 Tone bus would pull into town, with Madness making the most noise, and they'd set up stall. Every band had its good days and its bad days, but they were playing to packed houses who were too busy dancing to notice. Manchester's Apollo was the only seated venue on the tour, but even there the place erupted into a sweaty mass of dancing bodies.

Charley Anderson of the Selecter summed up the feeling on the tour. "What we're aiming for is a family of music, the Coventry Stax if you like. That is what 2 Tone is all about. The label says something. It has created an identity out of nothing. We're not aiming for competition. We're not going out to try and say that The Selecter are trying to run off The Specials or that Madness aren't as good as The Selecter. It's a matter of trying to present each band at their best."

The idea of 2 Tone as one big happy family suffered a set-back just a week into the tour when serious trouble broke out at Hatfield Poly. A group of about 30 blokes, who had previously been refused entry, smashed their way in through a fire exit during The Selecter's set and started slashing people with razors and Stanley knives. They were carrying banners announcing their entry as 'Hatfield Mafia' and 'Hatfield Anti-Fascist League' and made it obvious they were after National Front supporters, but as too often happens innocent by-standers were caught up in it all. Ten people ended up in hospital, 11 were arrested and about a grand's worth of damage was done (or at least that's the story they told the insurance company). All this kicked off in a room with a bar seperate to where the bands were playing, and The Selecter continued their set oblivious to what was happening.

Chrysalis played it down as a one off incident and the Specials' manager Rick Rogers was quick to underline 2 Tone's anti-violence stance. "Everyone on the 2 Tone tour wants to make it plain that they detest violence and those who come along looking for a fight are completely unwelcome at any of the gigs."

Hatfield wasn't the first bit of trouble on the tour and it wasn't the last, but it was the worst. Even so, the violence was more a symptom of the times rather than any reflection on 2 Tone. Gigs, particularly in the London area, were going off right, left and centre. Sham 69's Last Stand at the Rainbow that summer was more like General Custar at a Nuremberg Rally and there had been trouble at numerous other Sham gigs in and around the Big Smoke, as well as at gigs by The Angelic Upstarts, Crass, The U.K. Subs, Poison Girls and a lot more to boot.

A lot of trouble spilled over from the football terraces which had once again become a battlefield for the nation's youth. Football chants would go up and rival crews would end up fighting. Scores were settled, territories defended and bands followed, all in the name of a good punch-up. And London had more than its fair share of football firms at the time.

Cult violence was another aspect of the trouble that dogged the live band circuit throughout 1979. There were fights at mod gigs, punk gigs and the like, but most of the trouble seemed to be at gigs populated by the cropped hair fraternity. Skinheads fought skinheads over football, territory, politics, the works; and they took on all-comers for much the same reasons.

And then there was the politics. Extreme right-wing organisations like the National Front and the British Movement were enjoying considerable support around the country and in particular amongst young people. Both the NF and the BM were quick to court the skinhead movement for support, and skinhead gigs proved fertile recruiting and stomping grounds for them. While everyone else was attacking skinhead violence, newspapers like the Young National Front's *Bulldog* were glorifying it. And on the other side of the political coin were organisations like the Anti-Nazi League and Rock Against Racism, set up to combat the growing threat from the racists..

With life never being as simple as it's made out to be, there was rarely just the one reason for trouble at gigs, and no doubt there was many an occassion when people didn't even know why they were fighting. Drink is always a good talker too. The point was that people were going to gigs expecting and even looking for trouble and in that sort of atmosphere, they're bound to find it. And things weren't made any easier by the over-enthusiasm of some bouncers to start fights (in fact an organisation, C.U.R.B., was set up after a fan was killed at a gig not connected with 2 Tone by 'security').

2 Tone, despite its blatantly multi-racial stand, got caught in the firing line largely because of its skinhead following. The press can say what it likes, but skinheads and racism do not always go hand in hand. A lot of skins voted along traditional working class lines for Labour and a lot of others weren't interested in politics full stop. 1978 even saw the birth of Skins Against Nazis, something that took a lot more bottle than moaning on about the National Front from within the safety of a student Union. Even so the press somehow had 2 Tone down as a racist organisation at the start, with the *London Evening News* taking the biscuit with an article headlined, "Don't Rock With The Sieg-Heilers", above a picture of the multi-racial Selecter. Talk about missing the point.

Even so, there's no escaping the fact that large sections of some 2 Tone audiences consisted of racist skinheads. What's more gigs were leafleted by both the NF and the BM and their 'papers were sold outside. The fact that The Specials and The Selecter contained members that did not quite fit the master race stereotype was neither here nor there for most of them, but the band they really took to heart was Madness. Not only were Madness the only all-white band associated with 2 Tone, they also had skinheads in their line-up, and sections of their following took great delight in chanting, "Sieg Heil!", as they played.

At the time Madness front man Suggs said, "There's no way that we're political. We're certainly not fascists. If we were fascists, what would we be doing playing ska and blue beat? If we'd wanted to talk about politics we'd have formed a debating society, not a fucking band."

Not that it made much difference.

Prior to The 2 Tone Tour, Madness had played a handful of warm up gigs and there was trouble at a couple of them. At the Electric Ballroom on October 12th, Madness were top of a bill featuring Echo & The Bunnymen and another band that has always enjoyed a healthy skinhead following, Bad Manners. Manners opened and went down well, but skinheads in the audience prevented The Bunnymen from completing their set mainly because they weren't a ska band. Suggsy made a half-hearted appeal to the crowd to give the band a chance, but to no avail.

Madness were in a difficult position. It was their skinhead following who'd helped put them where they were and the band didn't want to turn against them, despite their warts and all. The music press was busy drawing battle lines and getting bands to speak out against the violence and the fascism. Rock Against Racism even had a go at 2 Tone for not doing enough to combat racism, but even a fool could see that The Specials on *Top Of The Pops* did more to promote racial harmony than a thousand RAR badges could ever do. Chas Smash put his foot in it a bit when he told *New Musical Express*, "They're just a group of kids, who, like any kids have to take their anger and frustration out on something. Some it's football, some it's music. NF don't mean very much to them. Why should I stop them coming to our gigs? That's all they've got."

Above: Rude boys return courtesy of The Specials,   Madness and a few mates.
(Source unknown)

Unfortunate it may have been, and the rest of the band were quick to distance themselves from the statement, but right or wrong it wasn't far off the mark. Mike Barson hit the nail even more squarely on the head when he said, "All that bloody right-wing stuff is just fashion. Half the kids down the squats at Kings Cross where I used to live are looking for a bit of excitement, they're just bored. One week they're in the NF, the next it's BM. If you try to have an intelligent conversation about it, they've no idea what you're talking about."

Of course you had your hard-core racists and always will have, but for a lot of kids, marching around school playgrounds chanting, "National Front!", lasted about as long as skateboards and pet rocks. Read all the sociology books you want, but that's the way it was.

Talk of Madness being forced off the 2 Tone tour by the trouble was nonsense too. It had been known from day one that they would leave on November 15th after the Scottish leg of the tour and be replaced by Dexy's Midnight Runners. After leaving the tour, Madness played a few more London dates and again there was trouble at the Electric Ballroom when the support band, Red Beans & Rice, were prevented from playing. Soon afterwards, Madness left for a low key tour of the United States and issued a statement as they left saying, "There is no way any of us is fascist - we are categorically against it."

In fact the problems with politics and violence almost caused the band to split. It wasn't that they didn't care, it's just that they weren't in a position to prevent it happening. Just because you can write and play good music doesn't give you a magic wand to solve the world's problems. "We're only in this game for a laugh," said sax player Lee Thompson while in America, "And if we are forced to drop out then none of us would have any regrets at all. We don't want anything to do with the National Front. As far as I'm concerned, if they start venting their political feelings at our gigs, then we can call it a day."

Back in old Blighty, the band's manager John Hasler summed up their position. "The band aren't in a position to issue an ultimatum, as that might just encourage people to wreck gigs, but I would think that if it got really heavy, they would jack it in."

The sell-out tour continued with The Specials, The Selecter and Dexy's Midnight Runners. Dexy's had been around since 1977, but it wasn't until 1979 that they finally got their act together, playing the youth clubs of Birmingham. However, it wasn't to the sounds of Jamaica that the band looked for inspiration, but to America and Sixties soul. They were accepted by the 2 Tone faithful for the most part and they were expected to be the label's next signing. However, at the end of the tour, Dexy's Midnight Runners flew in the face of predictability (as they were to do many times during a turbulent career) and released *Dance Stance* on Bernie Rhodes' Oddball Records label. A good song it was too, but without 2 Tone it sank almost without a trace. Later Dexy's Midnight Runners surprisingly rejected any association with 2 Tone, but went on to find success with classic cuts like *Geno* and *Come On Eileen* (both U.K. number ones).

"We don't want to become part of anyone else's movement", said Dexy's frontman and vocalist, Kevin Rowland. "We'd rather be our own movement.

"We were on The Specials' tour and we saw what happened to them. We're not interested in drinking or the best seat in the van. The most important thing to us is the show. And I've seen it happen to other bands. They're more interested in what's happening the next day or what's happening after the show."

The 2 Tone roadshow was proving an overwhelming success everywhere it went. It was as if a black and white chequered blanket was covering the country. And if there was still any doubters, all they had to do was to watch that bastion of pop music, *Top Of The Pops*, on November 8th. All three bands on the 2 Tone tour at the time - The Specials, Madness and The Selecter - appeared on it, as they celebrated their respective singles making their way up the Top Thirty. Walls really were tumbling down!

The end of November saw an emotional return to Coventry for The Specials and The Selecter as The Two Tone Tour arrived at Tiffany's. The gig was a 2,000 all-ticket sell-out and another thousand forgeries were floating around. Tiffany's was as busy as it had ever been and it was quite a contrast to even six months ago when The Specials were lucky to fill a Coventry pub. Like The Lyceum show a few nights before, the gig was recorded and a number of tracks were later to appear on The Specials' live EP released at the start of 1980.

As the tour came to an end, shows were selling out so fast that additional dates had to be added. The Lyceum gig sold out in hours as did an extra date there and in the end a third London date was added at the Lewisham Odeon, home of ska in the Sixties.

The year came to an end with a string of dates north of the border and two more sell-out shows at Tiffany's in Coventry, including an afternoon charity show for fans under the age of 16. To put the icing on a remarkably successful year, The Specials joined the big names of '79 including The Who, Queen, Costello, The Clash, Ian Dury, Wings and The Pretenders, for a series of charity shows to raise money for Kampuchea. Rumour had it that The Beatles were reforming for the show (the sort of rumour that knows how to shift tickets, but comes to nothing), but even without them, the fans were treated to the best of British, with The Specials blowing away an aging Who (a live cut of *Monkey Man* taken from the show appeared on the double album, *People's Concert For Kampuchea* on WEA).

It might have been a typically cold and wet winter, but things couldn't have been hotter at 2 Tone's H.Q. if it had been stuck in the middle of the Sahara.

RUDER THAN YOU

As was said earlier, The Selecter did not come together as a band until sometime after *The Selecter* appeared on the flip side of *Gangsters*. Neol (pronounced the same as Neil in case you were wondering) Davies wanted to form a band around the 2 Tone idea and Lynval Golding stepped in to lend him a hand.

"I was wandering around, wondering what to do when Lynval came along and pulled everything together for me, and it worked immediately. Three weeks later we were playing The Electric Ballroom."

Above: The Selecter
(Source unknown)

The line-up that joined The Specials and Madness for the 2 Tone Evening at The Ballroom saw Neol on lead guitar, Desmond Brown on keyboards, Pauline Black and Arthur 'Gappa' Henderson on vocals, Charley Anderson on bass, Compton Amanor on rhythm guitar and Charley 'H' Bembridge on drums.

All of them, with the exception of Miss Black, had been paying their dues on the Coventry music scene for donkey's years. In fact Neol, Charley Anderson, Gappa and Desmond had worked together in a band called Chapter Five way back in '73, with none other than a certain Silverton Hutchinson on drums. At the time they were playing a mixture of reggae and Booker T-style soul and never really got beyond rehearsing in the basement of the local youth club, but the seeds of '79 were already being sown.

"That was my introduction to reggae", said Neol. "Nobody white really understood the rhythm then. That period for all of us started off the idea of being able to mix what we had. I had only played in white bands before and they had only played with black guys, but we realised it worked so well, it was just very natural."

"When Neol came along and played some lead guitar I thought it was great, like Hendrix coming in over the top of reggae," added Charley.

Later Lynval Golding joined Desmond, Silverton and H in a band called Pharaoh's Kingdom which changed its name to Earthbound when Neol joined in the fun. When the band called it a day, Jerry Dammers borrowed Lynval and Silverton for his latest project, The Automatics.

By 1978, they were ready to re-group once again as Hard Top 22, yet another heavy reggae band. For the first time H dropped his bass in favour of the drums and Charley, Gappa, Compton and Desmond made up the all-important numbers. With five of the seven Selecters in Hard Top 22, it's a little easier to see how Neol managed to get a band ready for its first gig in three weeks flat.

At the time of Hard Top 22, Neol was marking time with The Transposed Men. Also in the band were Desmond, Brad (who was "'borrowed" by The Special A.K.A. for *Gangsters* and was never returned), Vaughan Tive who was later to appear in 2 Tone signing, The Swinging Cats, and a bloke called Kevin Harrison, who later had his 15 minutes of fame with The Urge.

The only missing face from the picture was Pauline. She had been working as a solo artist in local folk clubs, before joining Silverton Hutchinson and Desmond Brown (who seemed intent on appearing in every band he could on the 2 Tone family tree) around the time of Christmas '78, to lay the foundations of a new band. A band that was never to happen because Lynval told Neol to check out this "sensational female singer", and Pauline and Desmond joined Neol and Hard Top 22 to complete the musical jigsaw that was to be The Selecter.

Neol Davies was the only white member of The Selecter. His mother had died when he was only 11 and he was brought up by his father and his sister. To make ends meet during the years of going-nowhere-fast bands, he did any day job he could get his hands on. Dull office jobs, fork-lift truck driving, even cleaning toilets. Pauline Black was the only other member of the band born in England (Romford of all places, hence her London accent) and had a Nigerian father and a white mother. She was adopted as a baby by a middle-aged white couple and brought up in an almost exclusively white environment, where her half-cast face quite often didn't fit. She ended up at Lanchester Poly to do a degree in Bio-chemistry, but dropped out to become a radiographer at a local hospital.

Her real name wasn't Black at all, but Vickers. The problem was that in the early days of the band, she had to sneak away from her job as a radiographer to do gigs and she couldn't afford her real name to appear in the music press for fear of the sack. After rejecting numerous aliases, the band stumbled across Black and it seemed to fit the bill perfectly. So perfectly in fact that in early 1980, she changed her name by deed poll to just that. Pauline Black.

Neol might have been the only white member of the band, but to write off Pauline and the others as black would be to totally miss the point. The sort of dangerous generalisation that has every skinhead down as a brainless Nazi bootboy and every unemployed person down as a meaningless, lazy, scrounging statistic.

Organist Desmond Brown came over from Jamaica when he was a baby, but H and Charley didn't leave JA until they were eight and 11 respectively. It was a time when British businesses were advertising heavily in the West Indies for what was cheap labour to boost the size of the British work force. Charley's parents' left him with his grandmother in a village called Negril (now a tourist spot, but then a tranquil backwater with the only road in and out being a dirt track along the beach). When he finally arrived in England, his preacher father went to Brooklyn in the States, leaving his mother to cope with a large family. The streets of England certainly weren't paved with gold, and Charley's growing sense of frustration led to him becoming a rasta (by the time he teamed up with The Selecter, he was the proud owner of bright red locks). It was his way of showing the outside world what it was doing to his insides. Both Charley and H have fond memories of life on the tropical island.

"I was a rude boy even then," boasted H. "I lived over a dance hall in Kingston and I did my own hustling. I'd be outside the door and shake a leg and make a few pennies."

Gappa came to England from the Caribbean island of St. Kitts when he was 12, after also being left with his grandmother, until his parents had found a home and work. "In the village everyone knew everyone and there was a lot of discipline in that. If I walked down the street and I was swearing and one of my grandma's friends heard me, she would give me a clip 'round the ear. Then if my grandma found out about it she would give me a belting too!"

Compton wasn't from the West Indies at all, but from Ghana in West Africa. He moved to London when he was eight and then to Leamington when his black mother and white father split up ("A two tone idea that didn't work"). Even the band's white manager, Juliet Devie who was another import from Trigger, had been born in Trinidad and her parents' marriage ended in divorce too. None of them had the most stable of upbringings and yet in interviews all of them showed a sense of pride in their backgrounds and what they had been able to achieve. All of them shared a particular dislike for all things "middle class" and took particular delight in the fact that nobody in the band had ever been to art college. This sense of pride seemed to make them at one with their audience, who were mainly working class and beginning to feel the effects of growing unemployment and all the other rubbish heaped on the youth of any day.

"We're saying fairly heavy things like, 'Everyday, things are getting worse' and we're concerned and all the rest of it", said Pauline at the time. "That's something that people can relate to. There's no point sitting around like the punks did and getting completely depressed about the whole thing. What we're saying is, 'Bloody hell, you are having a bad time, but nonetheless you've got to see it through and somehow you're going to do it if you're in the right frame of mind to do it."

That was what 2 Tone was all about. Refusing to conform, refusing to end up on the scrap heap of life. Songs like *Rat Race* weren't an attack on those who had no choice but to work in boring jobs (whether we like it or not money makes the world go round), but an attack on those who fall victim to playing the promotion game and all its failings. And if an oddball bunch like The Selecter or The Specials could beat the system, anyone could.

Above: Birmingham's own, The Beat.
(Photo courtesy of Chrysalis Records Ltd. All rights reserved)

The success of The 2 Tone Tour pushed *On My Radio*, the band's first real vinyl outing, into the Top Ten and all was well. 2 Tone was functioning more along the lines of a family than a record label. It was run by musicians and not businessmen as everyone involved was keen to tell you. 2 Tone was a trading name of Chrysalis and there were no directors as such, but everything it did was decided by the seven Specials, the seven Selecters and their respective managers. And when other bands like Madness and The Beat were working with them, they too had just as big a stake in the enterprise as The Specials and The Selecter.

The Beat joined the 2 Tone family in October 1979. Life for the Birmingham band actually began in the Isle of Wight, when Dave Wakeling and Andy Cox found themselves there making solar panels, doing the odd bit of decorating, and sunbathing naked on the local naturists' beach, in the Autumn of '78. Both played the guitar and Dave liked to sing too. Neither were particularly good and Dave even played the guitar strings the wrong way round until Andy corrected him (he had copied the style of his childhood hero, Paul McCartney, who was left-handed and who'd restrung his guitar without having the decency to tell poor old Wakeling).

As much for something to do as anything else, they joined a band called Guyano, but quit a few days before the first gig. It wasn't really their cup of tea and anyway, they had difficulty playing the music. Instead they decided to form their own band and placed an ad in the local *Newport News* for a bass player.

The only person to answer the ad was a 17 year old punk called David Steele. In fact he hadn't been playing bass for very long and Andy had to write the notes of the guitar down for him. Some trio they made, but they were soon knocking out proto-gems like *Best Friend*, *Two Swords* and *Twist And Crawl*. Andy had David Steele down as "an odd little guy" and Steele had Andy down as "a northern weirdo" and Wakeling down as "a grapefruit salesman" because he always looked so healthy.

Things on the work front weren't very rosy and the two Brum boys decided to head home. As luck would have it, David Steele was about to embark on his training to become a mental nurse and he discovered that he could do the course at St. Alban's in Birmingham. So off they headed. The band still needed a drummer and after weeks of fruitless search, a nurse at the hospital suggested an excellent reggae drummer whose band had just broken up. Steele 'phoned him, and Everett Morton agreed to come along to the next rehearsal.

Everett Morton had moved from St. Kitts in the mid-Sixties, playing drums in the evening and at weekends and working in a kettle spinning factory by day. In fact he'd been playing with soul and reggae bands for some 15 years, including a stint with Joan Armatrading, before stumbling across these three angry young men. For some unknown reason, he joined the band after that rehearsal and another punk-reggae marriage was made.

Finding somewhere to consumate the marriage was not that easy though. They practised in Dave Wakeling's house and even at St. Alban's hospital (a move that caused the inmates much distress and almost cost Steele his job), before finally discovering the room above the Yorkshire Grey pub.

Steele believed that one gig would be worth a thousand rehearsals anyway, and despite the band being far from competent, he started pushing to do a gig. In March '79, he arranged for them to support a local punk outfit The Dum Dum Boys, at a local pub called The Matador. Two days before the gig they decided the band needed a name and after a quick flick through a thesaurus, they arrived at The Beat.

An eight week Tuesday night residency at The Mercat Cross followed and soon the band could count on a healthy support there. One early fan was a black punk called Roger Charlery, who went under the name of Ranking Roger. He was the drummer with The Dum Dum Boys until they split and then had a brief flirtation with a punk reggae outfit called The Visitors. However, he was best known on the Brum music scene for his toasting over records, particularly at Barbarella's where he was something of an attraction. He would often jump up on stage with bands to toast along to tunes, and had worked with two local reggae bands, Eclipse and a certain UB40. Roger knew Dave Wakeling quite well and it wasn't long before he was joining The Beat up on stage for the likes of Prince Buster's *Rough Rider*. And before you knew it, he was a permanent fixture.

The next few months saw The Beat playing more gigs in and around Birmingham with the likes of The Au Pairs and UB40, both of whom were also still waiting to be discovered. By then both The Special A.K.A.'s *Gangsters* and Madness' *The Prince* were getting regular airplay, especially on John Peel's show, and The Beat thought they'd blown it. Here were two bands playing a similar style of music and they both had a record deal. But all was not lost and it was John Peel yet again who was to give The Beat their first real break when they supported his Roadshow at Aston University.

It was the first time that The Beat had ever used a proper PA system and stage lights, and in front of a packed house of pissed students, they played better than they'd ever played before. Andy Cox reckons it was the best gig they ever played full stop. When they finished their set, Peel came on stage and said that The Beat were "the best band in the Universe after The Undertones", and said he'd spin a few records and then get them back on.

On The Beat came for the second time to repeat their set and pick up another three encores. Afterwards in the dressing room, Peelie couldn't praise them enough and made them swap the £360 he was being paid for the £80 they'd received. As they celebrated afterwards in a local curry house, the band were on cloud nine. That was until some bastard crashed into their hired van. You win some and you lose some.

John Peel asked them to do a session for his show and on air the following Monday, he kept raving on about this band he'd seen that weekend at Aston Uni.

The first link with 2 Tone was made in August, when The Beat were asked to support The Selecter at The Cascade in Shrewsbury. Afterwards they were offered any dates they wanted on The Selecter tour for petrol money and The Beat ended up playing five gigs with them. At one of these gigs, Jerry Dammers saw them for the first time and was very impressed.

The band then recorded a demo which failed to interest any record companies, but did get them more gigs. It came to the point where they felt if they really wanted to get on, they'd have to play London so off to the Big Smoke it was. Their first gig was at The Nashville, supporting The Selecter again, but it was a disaster for the Brum boys. Playing to an audience of mostly skinheads totally knocked them out of their stride. They'd played to skins before, but for some reason they didn't click with the London cropped ones. A few gigs on and things were back to normal. Backstage at an Electric Ballroom gig, Dammers asked The Beat if they would like to record a single and they readily agreed. A one-off deal was right up their street. In fact they had been toying with the idea of raising five hundred quid and putting out a single themselves.

For the single, The Beat chose to do a cover of Smokey Robinson's 1970 number one, *Tears*

Of A Clown, and one of their best originals, *Ranking Full Stop*. The choice of songs hinged around the Christmas atmosphere they would be launched into and the fact that they didn't really want to sign away two good originals to Chrysalis for five years. At first it was to be recorded at Coventry's Horizon Studios, but after a few technical mishaps, the band adjourned to London's Sound Suite. The producer was Bob Sargeant, a BBC house producer who'd done a good job on their Peel Session and who also happened to be the only producer they knew.

The band wanted to add some brass to the single in a bid for a more melodic sound. The answer came in the shape of a Papa Smurf-type figure called Saxa, a 50 year old veteran of the saxaphone. The old Jamaican had played with everyone from Prince Buster to The Beatles, but was now to be found playing jazz at The Crompton pub in Handsworth. Everett had worked with him on many occassions and it was him who took the band along to see Saxa in action.

Saxa agreed to play on the single and to do two gigs with The Beat before joining them in the studio. By then they were all getting on like a house on fire and Saxa was an honorary band member. When David Steele had asked Saxa if he wanted to know what key the songs were in, the old man had shrugged off the offer. "You just play and me'll blow. Me'll blow."

All of this was happening against a background of 2 Tone mania sweeping the country. The night The Specials, Madness and The Selecter were taking over *Top Of The Pops*, The Beat were playing to a full house at London's Rock Garden. As well as those sporting pork pie hats and DM boots, there were the by now usual assortment of journalists, photographers and record company representatives, taking in the latest 2 Tone offering. But such success was already creating problems. With both The Specials and The Selecter on tour it was becoming increasingly difficult to get hold of them, and when The Beat finally did get hold of Jerry Dammers, he wanted them to postpone the single release until the New Year. Chrysalis too said that there wasn't enough time to launch it on to the Christmas market, but with 2 Tone getting more coverage than the royal family at the time, The Beat kept pushing for the original end of November release date.

The Beat won the day, *Tears Of A Clown* (2 Tone CHS TT6) was released to a lukewarm reception from the press and went straight into the charts at 63. The band couldn't believe it! By this time every label in town was offering more and more money in a bid to sign them, with Virgin, EMI, Chrysalis, Warner Brothers and Arista leading the pack. One record company executive was even rumoured to have offered to double their best offer to date, without even knowing what it was. And this at a time when their top advance offer was £125,000! The band, helped by Dammers and friends, knew that big advances weren't the be all and end all of record deals and so held out for the what they really wanted.

"We decided that if anyone offered us a deal, we'd go for the same sort of thing as 2 Tone", said Dave Wakeling. "2 Tone did us a lot of good, so it would be nice to pass it on and do the same for other bands. We wanted to maintain our allegiance with 2 Tone, but having too many bands under the same umbrella could have allowed things to get sour."

In the end they plumped for Arista who gave them a £60,000 advance and their own label, styled on 2 Tone, called Go Feet. Such a deal wasn't new to Arista, who'd struck a similar one with Secret Affair and their I Spy label. The Beat contract was for five years and Go Feet was allowed to release up to six non-Beat releases a year. Negotiations with Arista took just over a month, but as soon as Chrysalis knew that The Beat were on their way, they not surprisingly stopped spending money on promoting the single. "They didn't even tell us we were on *Top Of The Pops*", said Dave Wakeling. "We found out almost by accident."

Even so, *Tears Of A Clown* climbed into the Top Thirty before the end of the year and peaked at number six in January 1980. Not bad for less than a year's work.

Above: More Beat
(Photo courtesy of Chrysalis Records Ltd. All rights reserved)

The media was going 2 Tone mad. A casual remark or the airing of a possible idea would immediately appear in the press as gospel. Like Terry Hall and Pauline Black teaming up for a single which never happened and was probably never really on the cards anyway. Similarly, any band playing anything remotely like The Specials was linked with 2 Tone. It happened with Dexy's Midnight Runners and before *Tears Of A Clown* was even on the shelves, the music 'papers had discovered the next big thing on the black and white label. UB40.

True, they did come from the Midlands and they did plough a similar musical field as the bands already on 2 Tone (UB40 were always a reggae band though, and never claimed to be a ska band), but their only real connection with the label was that they often appeared on the same bill as The Selecter and fellow Brum mates, The Beat. Fresh off the dole queue (the name UB40 was taken from the serial number on an unemployment attendance benefit card), this was the band's first taste of the music business, but they knew what they wanted out of it. After turning down various offers from major labels, including a £100,000 advance, they signed to a local independent label and formed Graduate Records. No advance, but a 50% royalty rate and total artistic control. But even this deal had its disadvantages. No advance meant that the band had to go into debt to buy the instruments needed for success and to record their debut single, the double A-sided *King* with *Food For Thought*. Even so, UB40 continued to find chart success long after the demise of all of the 2 Tone bands, and have the proud achievement of getting a truly independent single release into the British Top Five (it reached number four in March 1980).

Another band linked with 2 Tone was London's Bad Manners. Fronted by the larger than life Buster Bloodvessel of 13" tongue and 30 Big Macs fame, Manners were playing the small London pub and club circuit when The Special A.K.A. first came to town. A more oddball rabble of scruffs you'd be hard-pressed to find, but with songs about skinheads and being fat, as well as a wide array of covers from Bobby Picket & The Crypt Kickers' *Monster Mash* to Sam Sham & The Pharaohs' *Woolly Bully*, Bad Manners ranked alongside the best of 2 Tone in the live stakes. Jerry Dammers asked them if they would like to release a single on 2 Tone, but they passed up the offer and signed a deal with Magnet. A move that Buster, real name Doug Trendle, later admitted was a mistake.

"We didn't have a demo tape or anything, so we got one together, and by the time 2 Tone came back to us there were other companies after us", said Doug. "And because we thought 2 Tone was more of a stepping stone for groups who couldn't get a good contract, and we already had Magnet and others offering us a lot of money, we let it pass. And 2 Tone had only offered us a one-off single deal anyway."

The big problem was that things were happening too quickly and it was virtually impossible to put the brakes on and not get carried along with it all. Doug was only 19 at the time, so was Terry Hall from The Specials and Ranking Roger weighed in at only 18. What you had was a lot of inexperienced musicians, suddenly being thrust on to the centre stage and being asked to make decisions about their long-term future. And learning by your mistakes can be a very costly exercise, particularly in the music business.

After the success of '79, everyone was expecting great things of 1980 and the new decade. Coventry was being tipped as the Eighties equivalent of Merseyside in the Sixties, with 2 Tone already reaching Beatlemania proportions and people making jokes about 2 Tone being the best thing to come out of Coventry since the M1.

2 Tone had seen the New Year in with a gig at London's Dingwalls. The Selecter and a new all-girl ska band, The Bodysnatchers, were on stage and most of The Specials and Madness were dancing away in the audience. Such was the buzz about 2 Tone, particularly live, that even Lemmy and Animal from heavy metal faves Motorhead were there to join in the fun (despite his locks, Animal had actually been a skinhead in the early Seventies).

1980 began with controversy for 2 Tone at home, and The Specials jetting off for their first American tour.

First the bad news. Elvis Costello, who had produced The Specials' debut album, was having trouble releasing his own. At the time, Costello was signed to Radar which was suddenly closed down by parent company WEA, who then claimed the right to release Costello's work. For his part, Elvis had no wish to sign directly to WEA and argued that his deal with Radar was on a release by release basis. In fact he said that he would rather not release records at all rather than put them out on Radar's Big Brother.

Costello and his manager, Jake Riviera, then set about starting their own record label, F-Beat, which would kick off with Costello's new album, *Get Happy*. In the meantime, Jerry Dammers agreed to release a one-off single on 2 Tone, a cover of Sam & Dave's *I Can't Stand For Falling Down* with a Costello original, *Girl's Talk*, on the flip side (2 Tone CHS TT 7). WEA then went to court and won an injunction to stop 2 Tone releasing the single until the dispute was settled.

This left 2 Tone with 13,000 copies of the single ready to be released. In fact they were accidentally released, but quickly withdrawn. Capital Radio in London was playing the single from an acetate and rumour had it that the only reason the BBC weren't doing likewise was because of the threat of legal action. Copies of the single started changing hands at £75 a throw because people didn't think it would ever be released on any label.

By mid-January, The Specials were ready to release their *Too Much Too Young* live EP and knowing that it was unlikely that the Costello single would ever see the light of day on 2 Tone, the catalogue number was re-used for The Specials' release.

In the end, WEA relented and allowed Costello to pursue his career with his own F-Beat label ("The Stax to 2 Tone's Motown", as Elvis, a man who's always got a lot to say for himself, called it). The single eventually came out on F-Beat at the start of February and by the end of the month had reached number four. Most of the 13,000 2 Tone singles ended up being given away at gigs on Costello's U.K. tour later in the year. Towards the end of the year, a couple of thousand more were pressed with the 2 Tone label, but with both the 2 Tone and F-Beat catalogue number in the run-off grooves, and were sold outside Costello's 1981 concerts at the New York Palladium. For the collector in you, a copy of either will cost you an arm and a leg nowadays.

The good news was that after a handful of European dates, The Specials were on their way to teach Uncle Sam a thing or two about good-time dance music. When they arrived, *Specials* had just entered the U.S. Top 100, thanks to a big push by Chrysalis on that side of the Atlantic which was also to see the simultaneous release of the 2 Tone singles to date. There were so many requests for interviews that the band decided to hold a press conference on arrival instead. At the conference, a journalist asked The Specials if they would continue to play Jamaican music. "We don't play Jamaican music", replied Dammers. "We play English music."

The tour kicked off at Hurrah's in New York on January 24th where the band broke the house attendance record. The band went on stage two hours late which dampened the otherwise electric atmosphere, but they soon made amends with a 75 minute set that had the place jumping. The yanks might not have known much about ska music, but they certainly knew how to have a good time. Even Debbie Harry (surely the face of '79) was there to welcome 2 Tone's favourite sons to the land of Mom's apple pie and all that.

"This is our first ever gig in America", said Terry Hall as he fixed his glare on the assembled New Yorkers. "And we just can't say how pleased you must be to have us here!"

Terrance liked to use that as an opener, particularly at foreign gigs.

"This is it my little petals. This is your last chance to dance before World War Three!"

Every Specials gig was a party and this was no exception. Neville Staples running around like a headless chicken, Jerry Dammers vaulting his keyboards to join in, Horace, Lynval and Roddy all dancing away with their guitars as partners, and Brad just about managing to keep it all together with his hard-driven drumming. And in the midst of all the chaos, there was Terry Hall practising the fine art of standing still. No, not practising, because this was one art Terry had mastered to perfection.

Highlights of the rest of the tour saw The Specials blowing away The Police whenever they supported them, playing to 700 youngsters in the bible bashing, teetotal world of Oklahoma ("I really envy them", said Jerry. "Fancy being able to hear all that great music for the first time. The whole bit: ska, mod, great!") and a three day stint at The Whiskey club in Los Angeles. The club had been totally redecorated in black and white checks in honour of the visitors and it ended up more like a three day festival than a series of plain old gigs. "It's more like a holiday for us", commented Dammers. "Something to spend the money from *A Message To You Rudy* on."

But all wasn't milk and honey for The Specials in the land of the free. The level of commercialisation on the tour was a major problem. For all their efforts to beat the system in the U.K. (or at least use it to their best advantage), The Specials were at its beckon call in the States. The Specials weren't a band over there, they were a product. And they didn't make music, they made money by selling units of records. Maybe that's one reality of the music business the world over, but nowhere is the truth so naked as it is in the good old U.S. of A. At one stage, we weren't far off having a Jerry Dammers doll to take on Action Man and Barbie.

The other problem was the sheer size of the place, a problem that every band that tours there comes up against. Every state is the size of your average European country (often bigger) and more often than not the band had to travel hundreds of miles between dates. And once you've seen the four walls of a room at a Holiday Inn, you've seen them all. "Will The Specials break America or will America break us?", asked Jerry Dammers with a question that would prove more prophetic than he could have imagined in times to come.

"It's a weird life", said Roddy Radiation. "You spend all this time travelling and hanging about, just to spend three quarters of an hour on stage. That's what you do it for, but you have to put up with all this sitting around in a car or a van or a plane and feeling sick from a hangover or something."

By the time The Specials returned to New York for a farewell gig, a few members of the band admitted to be losing heart and they were certainly all glad to be back in wet and windy Blighty. "We were getting on each others nerves a lot of the time because we were stuck in a mobile funeral parlour travelling around", said Terry Hall.

In lots of ways that final gig summed up the tour. The show was at the Diplomat Hotel Ballroom on March the 1st, but tickets were priced at ten dollars - high even by American standards. As a result ticket sales were slow, while Madness, who were also touring the States at the time, could have sold out their gig twice over at a similarly sized New York venue only nights before. Articles even appeared in local newspapers, condemning the high ticket prices. It seemed strange that a band that sung about the rat race and concrete jungles would want to play in front of the city's affluent minority.

The promoter of the show was a certain Ron Delsener, a well-known figure in New York, who had most of the city's large venues sewn up. He also had a reputation for supporting guaranteed returns rather than new or up-and-coming talent. It wasn't the music that was important, it was the money, and that's exactly how it looked for this Specials gig. However, it was the fans who had the last laugh. A week or so before the gig, official-looking posters started appearing all over the city. They took the form of an open letter, supposedly from The Specials and apologising for the high ticket prices. It went on to say that as the band did not want to exclude any section of their support from the gig, they had managed to put aside 500 free tickets "for our poorer fans". All anybody had to do to claim a ticket was to 'phone one of the four numbers below and there they were for all to call. Delsener's office and private telephone number, the booking agent's number and the head of Chrysalis' number. There 'phones didn't stop ringing for a week!

Meanwhile, back at the Batcave, 2 Tone was going from strength to strength. Before leaving for America, The Specials had released their live EP, *Too Much Too Young*, and just to confuse the issue the band had gone back to using their old nom de guerre, The Special A.K.A. When the band officially became The Specials was never really clear. At first it was like a nickname for the band, one that very quickly stuck and was adopted.

Even more puzzling was the fact that A.K.A., an acronym for "as known as", was initially thought to be the music The Specials played in some unenlightened circles. Straight up! I remember walking to school one day and seeing a mod girl with a big 'AKA' patch on the back of her blue trenchcoat. When questioned, she was convinced that The Specials played aka (pronounced "acker") and not ska at all. She thought we were winding her up when we tried to tell her otherwise, and when you remember the large number of badges and patches on sale proudly boasting the 'word' aka, who could blame her?

Back to the live EP. *Too Much Too Young*, a shorter and more spirited version than the album cut, was recorded live at The Lyceum in London, as was the cover of The Skatalites' *Guns Of Navarone*. The flip side was recorded at Tiffany's in Coventry and was billed as a *Skinhead Symphony*, featuring straight covers of The Pioneers' *Long Shot Kick De Bucket*, Harry J. All Stars' *Liquidator* and Symarip's *Skinhead Moonstomp* - all skinhead faves the first time around.

It was the first 2 Tone single to be released in a picture sleeve and for the first time a 12" version was made available, albeit on Japanese import. Even so, live EPs did not have a reputation for chart success, but such was 2 Tone's grip on the nation, *Too Much Too Young* quickly climbed the charts and spent two glorious weeks at the number one spot.

The Specials were woken up with the news in Oklahoma City and most of them went straight back to sleep. What people failed to realise was that The Specials weren't doing this for money and success (although both have to be better than poverty and failure), but because they wanted to do it. Instead of a dream come true for Jerry, it was the realisation of one of his worst nightmares in many ways. The monster that he had helped create was now totally out of control. Of course he wanted people to like The Specials, but it was just that the more successful you are, the more you become trapped by the pressures of the music business. "I woke up with this 'phone call in America and I just went straight back to sleep. I just could not face it."

Too Much Too Young was as socially aware as any record that has topped the charts. It hit out at all the unwanted teenage pregnancies and in that sense was pro-abortion and pro-contraception. Subject matter that proved just a little too real for the good old BBC to handle. As it made its way up the charts and rested at poll position, it not unnaturally received a lot of airplay and made a number of appearances on *Top Of The Pops*, but to prevent it corrupting the morals of the country's youth, the programme controllers had a funny habit of fading out the "Try wearing a cap" final line of the song. Either that or DJs just happened to talk over it. A bit like football commentators do when you can hear verbal abuse from the terraces on TV.

Even funnier was how the Beeb was quick enough to climb off this particular moral hobby horse in pursuit of money. A song that obviously wasn't fit for the BBC's radio and television audiences still managed to find its way on to a BBC album, *The Best Of Top Of The Pops*. Such is the way of the world I suppose.

The popularity of the songs on the EP quickly led to a demand for the original versions, and the likes of Trojan and Island (who together owned most of the rights to old ska and reggae classics) weren't slow in responding. And the likes of Symarip's *Skinhead Moonstomp* soon found their way into the lower reaches of the charts.

2 Tone fever also helped rekindle the careers of stars of old. Laurel Aitken was back in the charts with *Rudi Got Married* (I Spy Records) and the recording careers of Desmond Dekker, Judge Dread, Prince Buster and others were resurrected with varying degrees of success. Laurel, the Judge and Desmond also went back on the live circuit and during 1980 top Jamaican artists like Toots & The Maytals, The Heptones and Jimmy Cliff were to visit these shores.

The Selecter were also having a busy time of it come 1980. Chrysalis had rushed the band into Coventry's Horizon Studios to record a debut album in a bid to cash in on all the publicity surrounding 2 Tone at the time. The first fruits of the band's labour were to emerge on single format in the shape of *Three Minute Hero* backed by the *James Bond* theme (2 Tone CHS TT 8). It received a surprisingly mixed reception from the music press - surprising because it was not as blatantly commercial as *On My Radio* and had a lot more to say for itself. Still the

first seven 2 Tone singles had all gone silver with sales of 250,000 plus a piece, and there was no reason why this classy little number shouldn't do the same. And, at the end of the day, the critics who really matter (the record buying public) gave it their vote of confidence and made it a number 16 hit.

The success of the single bodied well for The Selecter's album, *Too Much Pressure* (2 Tone CDL TT 5002), which was released on St. Valentine's Day. Taking in much of the band's live set and with the added bonus of a brass section and even a boys choir, *Too Much Pressure* was every bit as good as *Specials* and in places better. For some reason the soulful reggae ska of The Selecter seemed to have more depth to it than the punk ska of their 2 Tone counterparts. Versions of Owen Gray's *Murder* and Justin Hinds & The Dominoes' *Carry Go Bring Home* were also far less obvious choices for covers than say *Monkey Man* or *A Message To You Rudy*. What's more, The Selecter's real strength was in their musicianship and Neol Davies' songwriting. *Three Minute Hero* and later *Missing Words* might have been certainties for single treatment, but both *Street Feeling* and *Out On The Town* deserve just as much praise. All in, 12 great tracks that saw the album go straight into the charts and almost immediately turn gold. It peaked at number five and spent a very creditable 19 weeks waving the 2 Tone flag in the charts.

Despite its success and quality, the band weren't entirely happy with their debut album and once again it was the production that was the problem. The band had come across an album by Erroll Ross while over in Europe, and they liked what they heard enough to ask him to poduce the album. What's more, he was from Coventry so what else did they need to know? Perhaps the fact that the one album they picked on wasn't representative of Ross' work, and *Too Much Pressure* ended up more reggae-fied than the band might have wanted. It was still all a learning game and this one would just have to be chalked down to experience.

February 14th also saw the start of The Selecter's 30 date 2 Tone 2 Tour to promote *Too Much Pressure*. Initially it was to be along the lines of the highly successful 2 Tone Tour, with The Beat and The Bodysnatchers joining The Selecter, but that little package wasn't to be. The Beat had their own commitments now with Go Feet and pulled out of the tour to do their own, although they still managed to squeeze in a couple of dates with The Selecter. The Bodysnatchers also pulled out, this time over a disagreement with 2 Tone and a proposed single deal, but by the time the coach was ready to roll they were on board with the problem sorted out. However, The Bodysnatchers still had to be content with being bottom of a three band bill with The Beat being replaced by Holly & The Italians.

Holly & The Italians weren't a ska band, but their debut single, *Tell That Girl To Shut Up* (Oval) had been well received and was on the outskirts of chart success when the tour got under way at Derby's King's Hall. Two of the band, Holly Vincent and Steve Young, were from Los Angeles and the other, Mark Henry, was from Brighton, and together they kicked up quite a noise for a threesome. The music 'papers were calling it heavy metal punk, but post-punk pop would have been closer the mark.

Either way, it wasn't exactly the diet the 2 Tone faithful were used to and a few days into the tour it was obvious that the package wasn't working. The leather-clad trio didn't quite fit the picture and being sandwiched between two ska bands didn't really help matters. After trouble during their set at several venues, the band decided to quit the tour. It was a shame because they were a decent band, but you pay your money and you take your choice. 2 Tone had always enjoyed a cult following, but by the start of 1980 audiences were almost entirely composed of skins, mods and rudies. Trouble at gigs and the fear of it kept a lot of trendy punters away and there's little doubt that a hall full of skinheads and what have you can be very intimidating to an outsider (it would be a brave skinhead who would have felt at ease at a heavy metal gig at the time). This worked against Holly & The Italians, and tabloid newspapers like the *Daily Mirror* didn't make matters any better with the play school journalism that described rude boys and skinheads as follows:

RUDE BOY - Wear pork pie hats and trilbys. Follow ska music. Some are enthusiastic vandals.

SKINHEADS - Have convict style cropped hair and wear bovver boots. Dance the moonstomp to reggae music. Enjoy fighting.

Above: **Pauline Black and Gappa Henderson of The Selecter**
(Source unknown)

The Selecter were obviously upset that the band were forced to quit the tour and issued a press statement saying, "We are disappointed that audiences haven't been willing to give a different kind of music a chance. We think Holly & The Italians are a great band which is why we invited them on the tour in the first place."

After being verbally abused and seeing some of their fans attacked, Holly & The Italians were a little more pointed in their statement. "We are appalled at the narrow-mindedness of a fashion-following audience - and apologise to those of our fans who were kicked and intimidated by a mindless few."

Holly & The Italians then set off on their own Right To Be Italian Tour (even if they were lucky if they'd even been on holiday there), The Bodysnatchers moved up the bill and another Coventry band, The Swinging Cats, was brought into the lion's den.

Apart from that little problem, the rest of the tour was a great success as it weaved its way around the U.K. with a few Irish dates thrown in for good measure. The Selecter carried off the headline slot with ease courtesy of an excellent live show. Some people had The Selecter down as a morbid bunch, but they obviously hadn't seen the band live. All of the band jumped about on stage, doing their best to avoid Charley's swinging red locks. Pauline Black, once described as the most militant black woman singer in the world, stormed up and down the stage, conducting the audience into a frenzy of dancing. Petite, pretty and with the cheekiest of grins, they were putty in her hands. And all topped off with a pork pie hat.

"I was a bit insecure, and the hat was something to hide behind. When we started off, I wanted to be seen as someone who sang and wrote songs, not just tits and bum, and the clothes I wore helped to make that point. I don't mind being thought of as nice looking as long as they put the music first."

Another aspect of The Selecter s live performance was a staged fight between band members during *Too Much Pressure* (The Specials pulled a similar stunt during *Concrete Jungle*). The theory was that after having the frightening reality of what violence looked like brought home to them, it would act as a release for any tension in the audience and as a deterrent to trouble causing. Sometimes it worked and sometimes it went horribly wrong and actually incited violence. Still, it was different. And then of course there was the ritual 2 Tone stage invasion and a rendition of the Prince Buster classic *Madness*, a song that also found its way into the sets of The Specials and, surprise surprise, Madness themselves.

March saw what was to be The Selecter's last release on 2 Tone in the shape of the number 23 hit, *Missing Words* (2 Tone CHS TT 10). The track was taken from the album, but was re-mixed by Roger Lomas who had produced *On My Radio*. The B side was a live version of *Carry Go Bring Come* recorded live at the same Tiffany's gig as the *Skinhead Symphony* that appeared on The Specials' live EP.

And then April saw The Selecter depart from these shores to try their luck in North America with a two month stint that took them through to June. The tour followed much the same pattern as that set by The Specials at the start of the year. The Selecter weren't massive news in The States or Canada, but they were playing to sell-out crowds, playing two shows a day at venues that could hold around a thousand people a go. 2 Tone never created the same mass movement in the States that it created here, mainly because despite sharing the same language, the two cultures are quite different. For the most part, 2 Tone tended to appeal to America's bored middle class teenagers who could afford to rebel. Still, the band enjoyed the tour, despite all the travelling with an openly racist bus driver and the fact that they'd often find themselves sandwiched between a heavy metal band and a Miss Wet T-Shirt Competition or some similar nonsense. The tour certainly finished on a high note with a week of sell-out gigs in the 2 Tone stronghold of Los Angeles.

Back home, we had to contend with the invasion of The Bodysnatchers. The band had only played their first live gig at the end of November, but by the time they'd finished the 2 Tone 2 Tour (less than four months later) The Bodysnatchers had registered their first chart hit, had done a Peel Session, had appeared on *Top Of The Pops* and even better *Tiswas*, and were generally having a ball.

Above: ***The invasion of The Bodysnatchers***
(Photo courtesy of Chrysalis Records Ltd. All rights reserved)

The idea for an all-girl ska band came from Nicky Summers, a Londoner who made up her mind to form a band after seeing The Special A.K.A. on their early visits to the capital. "I saw The Specials last April when they were playing places like The Moonlight Club and The Hope

& Anchor. Everybody who went there was dancing. Nobody fought or posed or stared at each other. It was just everybody enjoyed it. If you go to a gig, no matter how good it is, you don't get much out of it if you just stand there. Even if a band is lousy, or just not very competent like us, you'll still get more out of someone like us because you'll be dancing."

To find like-minded women to join her she made an abortive attempt to join the all-girl mod pop band, The Mo-dettes, and then placed an ad in the music 'papers saying rude girls wanted. She ended up with little more than three months of dirty 'phone calls, but by September she had managed to piece together the best part of a band. There was her good self on bass guitar, a freelance illustrator from Oxford on keyboards by the name of Pennie Leyton, Sarah Jane 'S.J.' Owens, a fashion designer on lead guitar, a Dover lass Jane Summers (no relation) on drums, a 17 year old alto-sax player called Miranda Joyce and one Stella Barker from Scunthorpe on rhythm guitar. The only one missing was a singer and that vacancy was filled by the only black member of the band, civil servant Rhoda Dakar. Nicky saw her at a Selecter gig and thought that she would be ideal for the band. The fact that she said she could sing clinched it. Being a fan of The Rezillos at the time, Rhoda had a beehive haircut and when The Bodysnatchers were on stage she would claim to be the rudest of the rude girls because she had the tallest hair.

"I don't think we'd have joined a group, I know I certainly wouldn't have, if there had been men involved", said Miranda commenting on the all-girl line-up. "Boys usually start playing an instrument at about 14 or 15, and as we were all joining to learn as we went along, it would have made us look ridiculous."

The fact that The Bodysnatchers were all of the fairer sex didn't make them all men haters or raving feminists, in just the same way that nobody said that Madness or The Specials were all gay for being in male only bands. That's just the way they wanted it and if the music business wasn't so male dominated, an all-girl band wouldn't even raise an eyebrow.

The Bodysnatchers might not have wanted to be shown up in a band with male members, but they were certainly game enough to learn their trade in front of a live audience. When they took to the stage for the first time on November 24th at the Windsor Castle on London's Harrow Road, they were far from ready. Playing a set of mainly standard covers like Desmond Dekker's *007* and Dave & Ansel Collins' *Monkey Spanner* and *Double Barrel*, they were simply out to have a good time and to entertain the audience. And the bum notes, dodgy lead guitar and false starts only added to the band's appeal. Now and again it's great to be in a pub with a band churning out all the old favourites.

At only The Bodysnatchers' second gig, The Selecter asked them to play on their forthcoming Spring tour and very quickly there were more interested parties than skinheads at what amount to a handful of gigs before they went on the road with The Selecter. For the marketing men, women plus ska equalled money and plenty of it. Whether they liked it or not, The Bodysnatchers were almost immediately dragged into the limelight when they should really have been paying their dues on the small pub and club circuit. Knowing it and putting the brakes on however, were two different matters. The Beat's Dave Wakeling summed up the situation they faced. "Every record company's going fucking mad over this 2 Tone thing. Look what's happening to The Bodysnatchers. They're going to get killed because they're not ready for it. People are waiting for the 2 Tone mistake and it won't be long."

And The Specials' Horace Panter was thinking along similar lines. "I'm not sure if it's too early for some of the groups. Sometimes I get a bit worried. Like if we sign The Bodysnatchers, what are we letting them in for?"

Before setting off on the 2 Tone 2 Tour, The Bodysnatchers signed a two single deal with 2 Tone amidst the by now usual flurry of record company activity that surrounded 2 Tone-related bands. Even if it was too early, the band wanted to make the most of their chances and better sign to the devil you know than one you don't.

The band did a lot of musicial growing up on the tour and they were very well received in the main. When they were the opening act, their biggest problem was not enough people arriving early enough to see them, but once they'd moved up the bill and The Swinging Cats were opening, more people saw and appreciated them. While on tour, their debut single was released. Much of their own material wasn't really ready to go out on vinyl and so a cover of Dandy Livingstone's *Let's Do Rock Steady* (2 Tone CHS TT 9) was chosen. It was a live favourite and seemed a good choice. The B side was an original song, *Ruder Than You*, which became something of a rude girl anthem and was arguably better than the A side. Once again, the 2 Tone stamp of approval was enough to see it climb into the Top Thirty and peak at number 22.

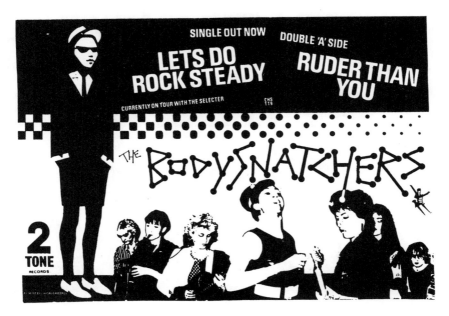

Such overnight success did have its problems though. Despite the hit single, The Bodysnatchers came off the tour completely broke. With the amount of money needed to keep The Specials alive and fed in the States (even with full houses, it was a loss-making exercise) and The Selecter at home, The Bodysnatchers just weren't a viable proposition for 2 Tone. They could have got money out of Chrysalis, but it would have meant signing a long-term contract with all the strings that go with it.

2 Tone was already starting to feel the effects of a media backlash and the inexperienced Bodysnatchers found themselves right in the frontline. It was 1980 and the media was already by-passing 2 Tone in search of the next big thing. The very same people who love to build

you up are just as quick and take equal pleasure in knocking you back down. Like vultures, they were waiting for the 2 Tone bubble to burst and they were quick to line-up the latest signing to do the dirty deed.

"If you're playing for fun, forget it", said Miranda. "Something popular and commercial doesn't prompt any interest, but you'll find Siouxsie & The Banshees and The Slits getting Record Of The Week, because if you're obscure and misunderstood artists, everyone sympathises."

The examples given probably aren't the best to illustrate the point, but there is nothing wrong with the analysis. Too many music journalists put themselves on a superficial higher plane than everyone else, and in this land of pretentious ramblings, good time dance music doesn't get a look in. The Bodysnatchers were an easy target when it was clever to knock 2 Tone. The band, who were called Two Tone Tessies, were the first to admit that they weren't exactly prime candidates for Most Talented Musicians Of The Year. And they didn't share the same cutting social voice that was the trademark of both The Specials and The Selecter, but they weren't 2 Tone clones either. For a start, their sound was nearer the rock steady mark on the spectrum of Jamaican music than any of the other bands, and anyone who wanted to write them off as superficial nonsense only had to listen to one song to know that there was more to The Bodysnatchers than was often believed. *The Boiler* (a song later recorded by Rhoda with The Special A.K.A.) took a no-nonsense story line route to portray the horrors of rape and it must go down as one of the most striking and horrifying songs you're likely to hear. There's no pretending that they were highly original and competent musicians, but at the same time they weren't just a bunch of pretty faces either. Sarah-Jane echoed this sentiment on behalf of the band when she said, "We're not women pretending to be men, but we're not the other extreme playing the helpless little girl game either."

Along with The Mo-dettes, The Bodysnatchers picked up a lot of respect from the rank and file when they pulled out of The Hastings Mod Convention because of the no skin/punk door policy. Given the level of inter-cult violence at the time, the policy was quite understandable, but it was good to see the band willing to put their principles before a pay day.

May saw the release of The Specials' *Rat Race* (2 Tone CHS TT 11) and in June The Bodysnatchers joined them on the road in England. The *Rat Race* single saw The Specials back in the Top Five and also saw them coming of age. Before, Dammers had done most of the songwriting, but *Rat Race* was penned by Roddy Radiation and the flip side, *Rude Buoys Outa Jail*, was a joint effort from Lynval Golding and Horace Panter. It obviously took some of the workload off Jerry, but also showed that other members of the band were emerging as more all-round musicians. The BBC were up to their old tricks again with the banning the video for *Rat Race*. In it, Jerry Dammers was dressed up as a fearsome schoolmistress and following its only showing on *Top Of The Pops*, the Beeb were apparently flooded by complaints from angry parents saying that Miss Dammers had scared their children.

The 12 day tour took in a dozen seaside resorts, but it wasn't as much fun as it might have been. Two days into the tour at the Sands Show Bar in Skegness, the stage collapsed because too many people had climbed on to it during a stage invasion. Luckily nobody was hurt, but someone could quick easily have been killed. "They just want to be part of it", said Jerry Dammers. "They're all really good kids."

Even the 2 Tone Birthday Party at The Friars, Aylesbury on June 12th couldn't fully lift the spirits in The Specials' camp. They were all feeling the worse for wear, particularly after

America, and there was quite a bit of arguing going on. Dammers had carried the 2 Tone cross for over a year now and it had both mentally and physically drained him. He and Roddy Radiation were at each others throats constantly, with one outburst occuring on stage in front of a full house.

"This band's falling apart at the seems and it's all because of your egos", said The Specials' manager, Rick Rogers, as he tried to see the band through the short tour.

There are always disagreements within bands and The Specials were certainly no exception to the rule. Work on their second album hadn't gone well and a proposed July release with full national promotional tour had to be postponed until September. At least it gave them a chance to catch their breath after a very successful year at the top of the rock n' roll tree.

2 Tone was shaping up to be the most successful label of all time in terms of consistent chart entries (including the likes of The Beatles' Apple label). Not only did other labels try to cash in with similar sounding bands, but occassionally by trying to sell them in 2 Tone style sleeves too. It was a cheap marketing ploy that was never likely to work to the full, but nonetheless it would certainly attract the eye of the right sort of punter who might still buy it.

The best known 2 Tone clone sleeve attempt was made by the Rocket label for the Brighton mod band, The Lambrettas. As a one-off, they released *Poison Ivy* on the 2 Stroke label which had an almost identical paper sleeve design to that of 2 Tone, except for the fact that Walt Jabsco had been replaced by a mod look-a-like complete with parka. 2 Tone gave Rocket permission to do it as a limited edition of 8,000 and it turned out to be a Top Ten hit for The Lambrettas. The band saw the funny side of the 2 Stroke idea, but after already copping it for jumping on the mod bandwagon, here they were getting it for this little effort. The sting in the tail was that it was their record label's idea and the man responsible, Peter Collins, had worked with The Specials when they were still The Automatics. It really is a small world.

Above: On the left is The Lambrettas' Poison Ivy, the most famous 2 Tone clone sleeve. And on the right is another example, The Charlie Parkies with The Ballad Of Robin Hood.

MISSING WORDS

July 1980. It was going to be one of those months. Exactly a year ago , *Gangsters* had hustled its way into the charts as 2 Tone made its first move in the world domination stakes. Only 12 months on and things were starting to go horribly wrong.

The first kick in the teeth came from the Greater London Council. 2 Tone had been planning to hold a massive birthday party on Clapham Common to celebrate its first year and The Specials, The Selecter, Madness, The Beat and The Bodysnatchers had all agreed to play. The local Lambeth Council had no objections and wanted to incorporate the party as part and parcel of their own summer festival of events, but no one had counted on the opposition from local traders and a vicar who feared for his stain glass windows (obviously a *Daily Mirror* reader). They petitioned the G.L.C. who then slapped a ban on the gig by refusing to grant a licence. An alternative venue in the Midlands was sought, but eventually the idea had to be shelved.

The Specials' July tour of Japan could have got off to a better start too. The land of the rising sun leaves even America trailing in terms of commercialisation as the band were about to find out. Where else in the world could you buy 2 Tone cigarettes for crying out loud?! And there were even comic books depicting kung-fu fighting between The Specials and Madness on sale.

The tour got off to a flying start in Osaka where a Brit-style stage invasion landed the band in a lot of trouble and their manager in a police cell for the night. It obviously wasn't the done thing in a land of weird and wonderful laws. The club manager wanted to turn off the power, but Rick Rogers stopped him and when the police arrived poor old Rick was carted off to the local plod shop with the gig promoter, who was deemed responsible for the invasion. The Specials had to stay in their hotel until the matter was resolved and it wasn't until the next day that they saw Rick Rogers again! A second Osaka date was cancelled, but the rest of the tour continued happily and without incident.

A chance for The Specials to let their hair down a bit should have come with the Montreaux Music Festival, where they represented Great Britain with the likes of Elvis Costello and The Q-Tips. A good time was had by all at what was rock's annual jamboree, but events were overshadowed by a vicious attack on Lynval Golding two days before they flew out. As he was walking away from a Mo-dettes gig at The Moonlight Club, three men beat him up and left him in the street needing hospital treatment. There was nothing to suggest that they knew who he was, and Lynval later said that it was a purely racial attack.

There was at least one light-hearted moment at Montreaux though. In the early hours of one morning, a couple of Specials drove a car right through a marquee full of sleeping people. In one end and straight out the other, with Dammers leaning out of the window shouting, "Morning campers!", to the startled faces peeping out of sleeping bags!

The biggest bombshell was yet to be dropped, however. The Selecter were not happy about the way 2 Tone was heading and told The Specials that they thought the label should call it a day while it was on top. When The Specials, and particularly Dammers, said they wanted it to continue, The Selecter announced that they were leaving the label. They then signed directly to Chrysalis and set up their own label, one without a name.

Things hadn't been right for months between the two bands. The problem was that 2 Tone had literally grown too big for its boots. The label worked well when both bands were on the same tour bus or even in the same country, but this was becoming the exception rather than the rule, particularly with both bands touring America at different times. "Contact with The Specials was interrupted all the time because we were in different places," complained Neol Davies. "So you lose that kind of understanding you start out with. It had become a hold back for us".

The Selecter believed that 2 Tone had become just too popular and in doing so had totally lost its way. There was no real master plan for 2 Tone at the start, but Dammers did have definite ideas about what it was to be. But events had quickly overtaken any philosophy and as the label became more and more successful, Dammers began to lose control. Within a year, 2 Tone had become a runaway nightmare.

"It's completely out of hand", admitted Dammers at the time. "2 Tone has become a monster, like Frankenstein's monster. There's such a danger of it becoming too commercialised. People don't believe us, but we'd do this anyway."

In 2 Tone, Chrysalis more or less had a free A&R department and a free quality control department. The rapid growth of 2 Tone meant even more work and most of it was landing on Jerry Dammers shoulders. What made matters worse was that Dammers wanted to do everything himself and came across as something of a benevolent dictator. It wasn't that he didn't trust anyone. He just lived by the theory that if you want a job done well you do it yourself. But with Dammers trying to do a good job for 2 Tone and for The Specials, too much was left undone, let alone done well.

"We didn't do anything bad", said Lynval Golding. "They had the freedom to do anything they wanted to do. But the actual running of the label got completely out of hand. A lot of things that should have been looked at weren't."

It wasn't even as if they were all making a fortune because they weren't. The Specials and The Selecter were on £300 a month each. Not a bad wage, but not the sort of figure that saw you putting your name down for a Roller either.

"If a 2 Tone record sells 100,000, which gets it into the Top Ten, I stand to make a maximum of £250 out of it," said Dammers. "2 Tone gets a 2% royalty and that's cut between eight people - it was about 16. That doesn't even pay the costs of running the 2 Tone office."

Despite their vinyl success, The Selecter were much better off financially signing direct to Chrysalis and in fact got a better deal than 2 Tone had. Walking away with £125 each after a chart hit and always having to play second fiddle to The Specials meant 2 Tone had become a liability for the band.

Confirming his worst fears, the monster that Dammers created had unleashed a level of commercialisation that tended to trivialise what the label was about. 2 Tone had depth and meaning, but it was turned into a fad by the marketeers and eventually dismissed as such. And as most of the merchandise was unofficial anyway, it was the pirates raking in the money, not the bands.

"We're pissed off with the rip-off merchandising that's been flooding the market", read The Selecter's press statement. "At least a lot of sharks will be left with 2 Tone Selecter badges and ties, which we hope no one will buy."

The Selecter philosophy seemed to be if you can't beat them and you don't want to join them, leave them high and dry. And they had a point. Everywhere you looked there were vast quantities of black and white clothes, badges, patches, ties, the works. I remember even going to a fair once and being given 2 Tone badges on one of those prize every time (as long as you don't want the big cuddly toy) stalls. I had about ten goes, pocketed loads of badges and then trotted along to the local cadet hall. The idea was that I would sell them to my mates and make a nice little profit. But when I got there I found half a dozen other people had had the same idea. Gits.

Even worse for The Selecter was the amazing amount of merchandise available with the band's name mis-spelt 'Selector'. In fact you were more likely to come across a Selector badge than you were a Selecter one, and you had to keep checking your record collection to make sure you had the right spelling to scratch on your school desk. It was all right for the music press to rabbit on about the level of commercialisation, but you didn't see them knocking back all those ads for dodgy ties and parka patches. What's more, music journalists were top of the culprits' list in the Selector game. Even today, it's amazing how many articles are written about some band called The Selector and if the only thing this book achieves is the correct spelling of The Selecter, I'll die a happy man.

Above: The two faces of 2 Tone. Terry Hall and Pauline Black
(Source unknown)

One of the original aims of 2 Tone was to encourage new bands and to give them a helping hand on the way to success. However, The Selecter believed that instead of encouraging new talent, 2 Tone was stifling it. Sudden success like that thrust on to The Bodysnatchers was not necessarily a good thing and, as the press statement continued, "plonking a new group in the Top Twenty isn't enough. Bands need a lot more basic help than that."

2 Tone hadn't exactly gone out of its way to release new bands after the initial burst of releases from Madness, The Beat and The Selecter themselves. Only The Bodysnatchers had been added to the roll-call. But again it boiled down to time and the number of hats Dammers had to wear. 2 Tone never even really started out to be a specifically ska label. It's just the way things turned out. Even The Specials were considering releasing a northern soul number after *Gangsters*. It was meant to be a way into the music business for exciting dance bands in a bid to take music back into the live arena, and it just so happened that the best dance bands at the time were playing ska.

"We can tell from the tapes sent to us that a lot of bands feel that to get a deal on 2 Tone they have to play a certain way", said Pauline Black, "and you're getting just a load of clone bands who feel obliged to make only a certain type of music."

There was something not quite right about what Miss Black was saying. Ska had been losing its flavour of the month appeal since the start of 1980 and both The Specials and The Selecter had been hinting for a while about a change in musical direction. And it was true that a lot of bands had picked up the ska guantlet in a bid to find success, but a statement like that showed both arrogance and contempt for the very bands The Selecter made such a meal about wanting to help. Was it that difficult to believe that some of those bands sending in demos were playing ska because they actually liked the music and not simply because they felt obliged to? And if so, what was so wrong with wanting to sign to 2 Tone? Maybe The Selecter and The Specials felt that they had some sort of monopoly over the music. It was almost as if 2 Tone wasn't the only one growing too big for its boots. BBC 2's *Arena* programme made a documentary about 2 Tone at the start of 1980 which showed Dammers throwing demo tapes all over the 2 Tone office. That little show of disrespect for the work of other bands didn't seem quite right either.

Pauline Black wasn't alone in the 2 Tone camp in voicing such sentiments. With hindsight, it is clear to see that 2 Tone, and in particular ska, were just phases in the careers of most of the people involved. Most went on to play other forms of music and a couple have even had the cheek to turn around and say that they never liked ska anyway. Everyone has the right to move on and good luck to them, but whether they liked it or not the success of 2 Tone, The Specials and The Selecter was founded on that three letter word that was becoming almost a four letter one in some music circles. Ska.

In the media backlash against 2 Tone it was the little bands that suffered most. By the summer of 1980, the music press had tired of "this 2 Tone thing" and was looking for pastures new. Rockabillies were tipped as the next big thing and then along came the new romantics. Rude boys had obviously had their time. Records by the likes of Cairo, Headline, The Gangsters, Akrylykz, Arthur Kay & The Originals and Mobster were written off before they were given a bloody chance. You didn't expect any more from the media, but you did from 2 Tone.

What ever the rights and wrongs of it all, The Selecter weren't prepared to stay with 2 Tone. For their part, neither The Specials or 2 Tone wanted to get into a slanging match with them. "We are sorry that The Selecter decided to leave the label", read the 2 Tone press statement, "But 2 Tone will still continue with the main objective of helping new bands. The Specials wish The Selecter well in whatever they do in the future, just like they did with Madness."

The Selecter had been earmarked as one of the big success stories of the Eighties, but after leaving 2 Tone it wasn't to be. In September, Charley Anderson and Desmond Brown left the band and formed The People and after the failure of the *Celebrate The Bullet* album to find any real success in 1981, The Selecter decided to call it a day.

July 1980. Just a year after *Gangsters* had hustled its way into the charts, the 2 Tone bubble had burst. Maybe Dammers was right. "Rock n' roll can't change anything. It's all capitalism."

ENJOY YOURSELF

Apart from all the internal strife, the summer of 1980 was one of surprising inactivity for 2 Tone. The delay with The Specials' second album didn't help matters and with The Selecter gone, it left only The Bodysnatchers and their second single, *Easy Life* (2 Tone CHS TT 12), to fill the void.

Easy Life showed how far the band had come in just a few short months, as did the faithful cover of Winston Francis' *Too Experienced* on the flip side. It was far stronger than their debut single and certainly deserved to go higher than the number 50 slot it reached. The problem was that nothing stands still, particularly in the music world, and 2 Tone's charm was beginning to fade.

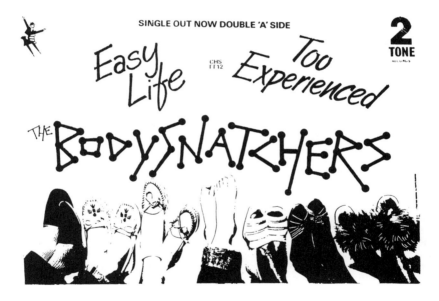

Specials' fans eventually had to wait until September for a sign of life from their heroes. The band began a British tour at St. Austell's in Cornwall on September 13th that kept them busy until the middle of October. The tour was to promote their second album, *More Specials*, which was released two weeks into it and a week after the release of the single *Stereotype* backed by *International Jet Set* (2 Tone CHS TT 13). *Stereotype* was about alcohol abuse and in particular one jack the lad type who pulled all the birds, could drink his age in pints and ended up wrapped around a lamp-post. It was certainly a departure from The Specials' usual sound and was their least commercial release to date, but just to prove they still had what it takes, it ended up reaching the number six position. In their infinite wisdom, the BBC decided that the record's content was too controversial for day-time radio play, when common sense suggested that such a message should have been played all day long. Still, who are we to reason why? We're just the mugs who pay the licence fee.

The change of musical direction with *Stereotype* (and *International Jet Set*) was to be a taster for *More Specials*, with both tracks appearing on it. The Specials had been playing the same set for well over a year and decided that it was now time for a change.

"You can't keep churning out the same old music as, say, Yes have for the last five years", said Horace Panter. "So the band's got to change and the thing is it's getting away from a formula that made us so popular. But now there are so many bands playing similar stuff, I think that's more reason to change."

Jerry Dammers certainly knew what direction he wanted to take to release The Specials from their ska straight-jacket. And the word was musak. A world of theme tunes and lounge music, a sort of soundtrack to people's lives. The music press lapped it up and were ready to champion it whatever it was. The thing about The Specials and Jerry was that people tended to take a lot of what they did far too seriously when they were really just taking the piss. And to your average punter on the street, this sounded like a wind-up, particularly when Dammers started going on about creating music for supermarkets and lifts. But, the man was serious.

"There's no such thing as good or bad music", argued Dammers. "I'd like to destroy people's ideas of good and bad music, so that eventually people will hear a record and they won't even know if they like it or not. That's my ambition."

However, not everyone in the band shared Jerry's enthusiasm for musak and in the clear light of day it did seem a bizaare route to take. Everyone seemed to agree that some sort of change of direction was needed before the whole show went stale, but they all had their own ideas about what direction to head off in. John Bradbury was still a big northern soul fan and Roddy Radiation was into rockabilly.

"There was quite a bit of disagreement in the band when we first started doing it", explained Jerry. "I just had the idea in my mind, and could see and hear it as a finished product."

In the end a compromise was reached. Part of the album would incorporate Roddy's and Brad's ideas and be closer to a more traditional Specials' fare, and the other part would be for more experimental musak. Despite the inclusion of tracks like the anti-nuclear *Man At C&A*, *Stereotypes* and *Do Nothing*, *More Specials* (2 Tone CHR TT 5003) was far more relaxed and far less angry an affair than the band's debut LP. The Specials were growing up and in doing so had lost much of their cutting edge. Ska had taken a definite back seat and punk had been thrown completely out of the window. Even the colour cover shouted mellow at you and was in sharp contrast to the stark black and white cover of *Specials*.

Even so, lift music it was not. *Holiday Fortnight* could easily have passed as background music for a Caribbean cruise TV commercial and *Enjoy Yourself* would go down a treat on a church outing, but the album was still very much The Specials. Even Brad's soul number *Sock It To 'Em J.B.* and Roddy's rockabilly *Hey Little Rich Girl* sounded surprisingly good after a strictly ska diet. In fact those who enjoyed a bit of rockabilly were in for second helpings thanks to a free single that was given away with the first 100,000 albums. The single featured two tracks that wouldn't fit on the album; Roddy Radiation & The Specials with the 'billy *Braggin' & Tryin' Not To Lie*; and a 90 m.p.h. re-working of *Rude Boys Outa Jail* courtesy of Neville 'Judge Roughneck' Staples. There was even a free poster for the early birds, featuring a picture of The Specials taken from the same photo session as the album cover.

This time The Specials chose to do their own production with the help of studio engineer, Dave Jordan. The album was recorded in stages over the summer of 1980 and proved a real family affair with guest appearances from Madness' Kix Thompson, Bodysnatcher Rhoda Dakar and backing vocals from The Go Gos, a band The Specials had met on their American tour.

More Specials was released at the end of September and went straight into the charts. It spent a total of 13 weeks there and reached number five. The music press loved it, but it received a mixed reception from the band's fans, many of whom were disappointed with the change of direction. Musak Skins didn't really have a ring to it. Still, at least a new album meant that The Specials would be out on the road to promote it.

Delays in the album had obviously delayed the tour and it's unlikely that the band would have toured if it had not been necessary to promote the album. Dammers was totally shattered and needed a month's rest rather than a month's hard slog around the country. The two weeks of rehearsals for the tour turned into a shambles, with Jerry being missing almost on a daily basis. And hours before the tour was due to get underway, Dammers asked to see a doctor who told him he was suffering from mental and physical exhaustion. Deep down, Jerry hoped he had some dreaded disease so that the tour could be cancelled, but at the same time he knew he would be up there with the rest of the band and the tour went ahead. Gigging was once the highlight for The Specials and now it felt too much like hard work.

The support band for the tour came in the shape of The Swinging Cats. They had been given their first real break when they replaced Holly & The Italians on The Selecter's March tour. Ironically enough, The Swinging Cats also signed a one single deal with 2 Tone only weeks after The Selecter had quit the label because of 2 Tone's supposed failure to aid and abet new talent.

The Swinging Cats hailed from Coventry and had started out on the musical trail at the end of 1979. Apart from sharing The Specials' home town, the only real connection with 2 Tone was guitarist Steve Vaughan's uncanny resemblance to Jerry Dammers. Both had a bumbling personality and both had no front teeth. A motorbike accident had removed half of Vaughan's, while Jerry, who had known his look-a-like from school, had fallen off a bike as a kid. Jerry's surviving pegs had been helped on their way by a beer glass later on in life.

"It was dead funny, when I fell off my bike", recalled Dammers. "I crawled into this house all covered in blood and 'phoned my Mum. She sounded dead shocked and horrified, but her voice sounded a bit odd. Then I realised I'd dialled the wrong number!"

Enough of Jerry's masochistic tendencies for the moment and back to The Swinging Cats. Although the band had a slight ska tinge to it, their biggest claim to a spot on 2 Tone was the fact that they played good time dance music. Ska, latin, calypso, it was all there in a nostalgic cocktail mixed especially for the danceable Eighties. They also had something of a fetish for Sandy Shaw covers and theme tunes along the lines of *The Avengers* and *Captain Scarlet*. The sort of fun band that would perhaps go down better at a student ball than a skinhead bash, and not surprisingly a band that had influenced Dammers' musak ideas.

"Hopefully the music stands up on its own as a variation on the 2 Tone theme", said Vaughan. "I think people will obviously get into it because of the 2 Tone thing, but we hope that they'll take it for what it is after that."

That might have been the game plan, but unfortunately the match didn't go quite as hoped. Having a stable line-up would have helped, but The Swinging Cats ended up going through more band members than England's had cricket captains. By the end of The Selecter tour, half of the band had left and been replaced, including the lead singer, Val, who had been going out with Jerry Dammers. The band soldiered on, picking up support slots with bands like Bad Manners and The Bodysnatchers and then in August, they headlined their own short tour of small clubs in London and the Midlands. By the time The Specials tour came around, the band was a six piece combo of Vaughan Tru on guitar, Jayne De La Swing on vocals, Toni El Dorko on keyboards, drummer Dicky Doo, percussionist Craig Guatamala and Paul Heskatt (made up name if ever I heard one) on sax, a man who had also found his way on to the *More Specials* album.

"Actually we want to make the sort of music you'd listen to while waiting for an ice-cream at the cinema or in a dentist's waiting room", said Vaughan. "Having your teeth out needn't be so painful with The Swinging Cats."

Left: The Swinging Cats. Above: The Cats' at The Ballroom. The Reluctant Stereotypes were always linked with 2 Tone and The Lemons signed to Brad's Race Records

The single, the self-penned *Away* with an old swing medley called *Mantovani* was released to coincide with the September tour, but unfortunately became the first 2 Tone single to miss the charts completely. And that despite the first 20,000 copies being sold at the special price of 50p. Now that it's rather trendy to be the discoverer of forgotten gems, *Away* is often held aloft as the one that got away. *Mantovani* was pleasant enough, but the truth was that *Away* did not do the band justice and sounded like third rate indie pop. It was neither liked by the press or the public and really didn't deserve to chart. *New Musical Express* summed it up rather nicely with the question, "Is the 2 Tone quality control on holiday or what?"

The next single on the chequered label was Rico's *Sea Cruise* with The Folk Brothers' 1962 Blue Beat hit, *Carolina* on the B side (2 Tone CHS TT 15), which was released in October. Now here was a real gem, but it's instrumental nature (Rico preferred to let his trombone do the talking) meant that it was never really destined for chart success. Despite the exposure he'd been given by working with The Specials, Island surprisingly did not renew his contract when it expired in January 1980, leaving him free to record for 2 Tone. They did make a half-hearted attempt to get The Specials to back Rico on a live take of *Guns Of Navarone* to be released on Island, but nothing came of it and so that was that. Along with Dick Cuthell, Rico had joined The Specials on their tour, but he missed a couple of gigs to fly to his native Jamaica to play at the Independence Day celebrations. But back in Old Blighty, the party atmosphere on The Specials' tour was about to be brought to an abrupt end.

IT DOESN'T MAKE IT ALRIGHT

The Specials were in their element on stage in front of an audience and they were also at their best. They hated the barriers that the music industry continually erects between artists and their fans, and gigs gave them the only real opportunity to be at one with their followers. And from day one, The Specials had allowed fans to join them on stage for songs, particularly the encores.

"Who am I to say they can't come up on stage?", Terry Hall had once said. "They've paid their three pound. They can do what they like as far as I'm concerned."

Even so, things began to get a bit out of hand during the More Specials Tour. Stage invasions were starting far too early in the set, often preventing the band from playing and forcing them to keep stopping to clear the stage. For those who clambered up with their heroes it was a moment of glory, but for the band it was becoming a little tiresome no matter what they said to play it down. It wasn't much fun for the rest of the audience either, who had to be content with playing spot the Special and watching broken performances. Stages were being built on different levels so that the band could retreat to higher vantage points, but they were still reluctant to stop stage invasions altogether.

"If we have to, we'll just have layers of risers, so we can just retreat backwards all the time!", commented Dammers.

Stage invasions weren't the worst of it though. The violence that had marred The Two Tone Tour had returned to haunt The Specials once again. Serious outbreaks occured at Newcastle and Cardiff, while in Edinburgh free drinks and records prevented the venue erupting into pandemonium during a 20 minute power cut. But it was at Cambridge on October 9th that things really came to a head.

3,500 people packed into a huge tent that was pitched on Midsummer Common to see The Specials. Trouble started early on when about 30 to 40 ticketless youths managed to force their way in, chanting "United!" and "Coventry, where are you?" as they did so. Fighting and can throwing constantly interrupted The Swinging Cats' set and the band's then vocalist, Chris Long, ended up getting involved in it all. He challenged the trouble makers to come up on stage to fight him if they wanted to fight anyone - and immediately a bloke took him up on the offer.

The Swinging Cats were forced to cut their set short and the arrival of The Specials on stage seemed to calm things down, but not for long. They said they would go off as soon as trouble started and after having to do so for the third time, The Specials said they wouldn't be coming back on. That was the cue for hundreds to leave, but with the threat of a riot on their hands The Specials had no option, but to go on stage yet again. By now the situation was hopeless, the police had been called and rather than helping the situation, bouncers were lashing out at anyone. Before abandoning the stage for the final time, Terry Hall had to be restrained after he picked up a microphone stand in a bid to settle an argument he was having with a bouncer.

In the dressing room, Jerry Dammers and Terry Hall were surprised to be told by the promoter that he was holding them responsible for the trouble and both were later charged by the boys in blue. Using threatening words and behaviour likely to lead to a breach of the peace it said on the charge sheet. It had been serious, but as usual it was blown out of all proportion, particularly in the local 'papers. One local councillor even claimed that The Specials planted people in the audience to provoke trouble as a publicity stunt and that the violence was all part of the show! In court, two bouncers and three police officers gave evidence against them and Dammers and Hall were found guilty and fined £1,000.

"When the tour finishes, we start really thinking about what we want to do", said Jerry. "I'd hate to be in a band that just churns out the same thing and no one else in The Specials wants to get involved in that. If we do something else as a band after this, it will be totally different."

The possibility of The Specials calling it a day showed just how serious things were getting. Touring was now becoming a chore and there was talk about playing only selected weekend gigs. They certainly didn't need the violence at live shows, but at the same time still didn't want to turn the stage into an impregnable fortress against their fans. Whatever was to be decided, one thing was for sure. The band needed a rest before considering their position in the rock n' roll circus.

One gig that they had planned to play before going into hibernation was at the Campaign for Nuclear Disarmament's rally at London's Trafalgar Square set for the end of October. Up to 100,000 people were expected, but when the Department Of The Environment refused to grant permission for the use of a giant P.A. system, C.N.D. pulled The Specials. Smaller bands still played with smaller rigs on the backs of lorries, but The Specials weren't even asked if they would be prepared to do that and it caused a bit of ill-feeling.

But a reminder of times gone by did come on the last weekend in October when The Specials joined Madness, The Damned, Bad Manners and Ian Dury & The Blockheads at the Hope & Anchor. The charity Blanket Coverage was holding a two day event to raise money for fuel bills and bedding for the capital's homeless and elderly. The atmosphere was totally relaxed and had The Specials longing to go back to the days when they were playing little clubs like the Chesterfield Fusion and Sheffield's Limit Club.

"I had this mad idea of going out and playing a completely new set under a different name", said Horace Panter with an idea that probably made more sense than gigging night after night as The Specials.

The Swinging Cats didn't even make it to the end of the More Specials Tour. They had been given a gigantic leg up by 2 Tone, but the instability of the band meant they ended up lucky to stay on their feet. The poor reception on the tour, the dismal failure of the single and the general pressures of the music pressures saw The Swinging Cats throw the towel in. And it wasn't long before they were joined in the proverbial early bath by The Bodysnatchers.

After the release of *Easy Life*, the band toyed with the idea of recording a debut album, but it never got beyond the planning stage. September saw Toots & The Maytals pay their first visit to Britain since they toured back in '76 with The Heptones, and The Bodysnatchers were lucky enough to pick up the support slot. October, and the band were playing their own headlining tour, but at the end of it the band split. The Bodysnatchers played their last gig at Camden's Music Machine at the end of the month and that was that.

Four months earlier, drummer Jane Summers had left to complete her education and had been replaced by Judy Gray Parsons. Even then things weren't quite right. For some time,

Rhoda Dakar and the band's founder Nicky Summers had wanted the band to take a more serious approach to music by adding the same sort of political edge that was The Specials and The Selecter. They decided to leave after the band had had one argument too many and when it became obvious that no one else shared their aspirations. The rest of the band just wanted a good time as was clearly illustrated by their next project, The Belle Stars. In 1981, this new tattoo and tights outfit signed to Stiff and released a couple of singles, the first of which, *Hiawatha*, could be found on an earlier Bodysnatchers' demo.

The feeling was that both The Swinging Cats and The Bodysnatchers just weren't ready for the pressures at the top of the music tree. They'd been given the opportunity to run with the big boys when they'd barely been able to walk.

"Take The Specials", explained Lynval Golding. "We went through the whole lot. We went from pleading with bands for a support slot, we went the whole road. We didn't form the band one month and suddenly we were a hit. With The Bodysnatchers and The Swinging Cats, they didn't have to go through it really. To me, I think The Swinging Cats were just lazy anyway."

That just left The Specials and Rico to hold the 2 Tone fort. In December, *Do Nothing* was re-mixed with the addition of The Ice Rink String Sounds, and released as a single with a suitably up-dated version of Bob Dylan's *Maggie's Farm* (2 Tone CHS TT 16). It was one of The Specials' best offerings and fully deserved its number four chart placing.

Besides the single however, 2 Tone was conspicious by its absence. The Specials had decided to take the six months after the tour at a less frantic pace, which gave everyone the chance to put their feet up and try their hand at other things. Jerry started work on the long awaited 2 Tone film, *Dance Craze*, and joined Brad and Horace making up the numbers in Rico's backing band.

Brad also started his own record label, Race Records. He had wanted to start one ever since being fascinated by the small indie labels he dealt with while working at Virgin. Rick Rogers looked after the business side and Spartan handled distribution. Even Lynval eventually got in on the act by doing some production work for Race signings, The People.

The first release for Brad's new label was *Moving To Rhythm* by the soul band, Team 23, who had picked up where The Swinging Cats left off at the end of The Specials' tour. That was followed by *Just Enough* by Night Doctor, a reggae outfit that could boast of having ex-Wailer Vin Gordon in its line-up. Brad actually came across the band by accident while appearing on Radio One's *Singled Out* show. While reviewing Night Doctor's *Music Like Dirt* (Copasetic), John started going into one about how reggae was always marginalised and in all the excitement he then proceeded to mis-pronounce the label the single was on. The band got in touch to correct him and that was when he asked them to record for Race. And his next signing was The People, the band formed by ex-Selecters Desmond Brown and Charley Anderson, and with another old face behind the drum kit, Silverton Hutchinson. Their single *Musical Man* was done as a tribute to the one and only Rico Rodriguez, but like the other Race releases, enjoyed little in the way of commercial success.

Race Records also released *My Favourite Band* by the pop ska band, The Lemons, a band that was to see a couple of its members go on to find fame and fortune with The Pogues.

Neville also started to play the own label game as well as working with his own Jah Baddis Sound System. Inspired by reggae greats like Joe Gibbs and Big Youth who were both producers and label owners, Staples formed the Shack label. A real family affair it was too, with girlfriend Stella Barker of Bodysnatchers and Belle Stars fame handling the marketing. And Shack signing, 21 Guns who released the excellent single *Ambition Rock*, had been formed at the end of The Specials' U.S. tour by two of the band's roadies, Johnny Rex and Trevor Evans. Neville and Stella had high hopes for the label, but it wasn't to be. Singles by Lieutenant Pigeon (*Bobbin' Up 'N Down Like This*) and Eddie Peters (*The Wonderful World Of Radio Wrappin'*) joined the 21 Guns' effort in the bargain buckets soon after release.

The Specials still continued gigging, but they were now picking and choosing the dates they played. January saw them play three dates in Northern Ireland and Eire with The Beat to raise money for children's charities and anti-nuclear groups. The gigs went well enough, but all £8,000 takings were confiscated at the airport as the band passed through Irish customs on the way home. Airport officials confiscated the money because such a large quantity broke Irish currency export laws. The Specials didn't have a clue about the laws, but very few countries allow such quantities to leave their borders. So the bands went home without a penny towards their expenses and the charities didn't benefit either.

Other gigs included one at a secret venue for Leamington Anti-Racist & Anti-Fascist Committeee in April and one in London to greet the May Day unemployment march from Liverpool (The Jam had seen them on their way). The Specials also played three outdoor gigs in as many weeks at the end of June and start of July.

The first was at Coventry's Butts Athletic Stadium with Hazel O'Connor, The Bureau (ex-Dexy's Midnight Runners for the most part), The Reluctant Stereotypes and The People. An Asian student had been murdered in a racial attack in the city and the gig was a benefit for his family. A proposed National Front march through the city on the same day was banned, and expecting trouble, the police were out in force at the gig. In the end there was no trouble, but the fear of it obviously contributed to the fact that the stadium was only half-full.

The following week, The Specials played a free gig in Rotherham at the Herring Thorpe Playing Fields and then it was on to the Northern Carnival Against Racism at Leeds. It was the largest event that Rock Against Racism and the Anti-Nazi League had organised for a couple of years and supporters were bused in from all over the country. About 15,000 people turned up to see a somewhat lack-lustre performance by The Specials, but it was the thought that counted. The NF could only muster a couple of hundred to march through Leeds city centre, but the carnival took on extra significance when people opened their morning 'papers.

The night before Leeds, there had been rioting in the streets of Southall, following an Oi! gig in the town. With 2 Tone now in rapid decline, everyone was looking for the next big thing, but rather than wait, *Sounds* decided to create its own. Oi! was working class punk that went back to the streets of '76 for its inspiration, not the art colleges of '77. Most of the bands labelled Oi! by *Sounds* had been quite happy to bob along under the ailing punk banner beforehand. Apart from *Sounds*, which always seemed the most street oriented music 'paper anyway, the media tended to treat Oi! with derision, with *The Evening Standard* calling it "pop's lowest common denominator". But the Oi! movement couldn't care less. It had found a home in the heart of the skinhead movement.

Southall on the outskirts of West London was home to a large Asian community and large numbers of its youth took exception to a skinhead gig taking place in their area. The Union Jack-clad bootboys were seen as some sort of threat to their community, mainly because your average punter knows no better than to equate skinheads with a modern day Hitler Youth. There had been talk of a confrontation as soon as the gig at the Hambrough Tavern featuring

The 4-Skins, The Business and The Last Resort was announced. 400 skinheads from all over London travelled to see their heroes and on the way to the gig there were isolated incidents between skinheads and local youths, but nothing to justify what followed. Halfway through the gig, 2,000 young Asians gathered outside the pub and started putting the windows in. At first the police turned up at the wrong pub, but eventually managed to ferry the bands and their followers to safety. The rest of the night was spent with running street battles between local youths and the police and The Hambrough Tavern ended up being burned to the ground.

There was no doubt fault on both sides, but the same old distorted half-truths from the nation's media came out. They were as quick to pander to the Asian community as they were to chastise the skinheads. And that's no Front rhetoric. Despite the picture painted by the likes of the tabloid press, the Oi! movement was more about having a laugh than saluting Hitler. A small minority of racists tried to infiltrate it just like they did with 2 Tone, but that didn't make either movement fascist. And if the skinheads had gone to Southall looking for trouble, they wouldn't have taken women and children along with them. As for the Union Jack ("They must be Nazis - one's wearing a Union Jack t-shirt"), the National Front hadn't bought the rights to it and it remained a symbol of national pride for most skinheads. In fact the very same symbol that had seen Hitler, Mussolini and their sidekicks on his way forty years before.

Even if The Specials weren't overdoing the gigging bit, you could always console yourself with a visit to your local fleapit to see *Dance Craze*.

There had been talk of a 2 Tone film for some time, but that's all it seemed to be. Talk. Originally it was scheduled for an end of summer 1980 release and then a December release, but both came and went and still no sign of it. January 1981 though, and it was previewed at the annual Midam music festival in France and in February it went on general release in Britain. February 15th saw *Dance Craze* open at Sheffield, Leeds and Manchester Odeons and over the following weeks it was shown at 36 towns and cities across the country.

Dammers, with his interest and background in film-making, had thought about making a 2 Tone film, but the idea for *Dance Craze* came from an American, Joe Massot. Massot had been making music films since the early Sixties, but the first time he heard the word ska was when he bumped into Madness by a hotel swimming pool during the band's first U.S. tour. That night he saw them live in Los Angeles and was totally knocked out by them.

At first he was only interested in making a film about Madness, but when his son told him about the 2 Tone movement and bands like The Specials, The Beat and Bad Manners, Massot broadened his horizons. He visited England where he saw the bands playing live and witnessed the effect that they were having on the British music scene. This was something that had to be captured on film. The plans for *Dance Craze* were made and Massot and his team started filming Britain's top ska bands at gigs around the country. From the mass of footage shot, 27 songs performed by six bands were chosen. The Specials, Madness, The Beat, Bad Manners, The Selecter and The Bodysnatchers were to be immortalised on celluloid.

Dance Craze made no attempt to interview the bands or discover the philosophy behind the bands. It was simply a case of capturing the British ska scene as it was happening and transferring the live buzz of a ska gig on to a cinema screen. There were two uninterrupted sets by the bands performing live favourites (including The Bodysnatchers' version of *007* which was never released on vinyl), with a middle section of vintage dance crazes like The Locomotion, The Twist and The Bosa Nova. Straight out of the black and white archives and complete with the silly BBC English voice-overs, this section was the perfect excuse to run out and buy an ice-cream before rejoining your mates for the second half. The entire film was shot on location at gigs, except for the mock fight scene during The Selecter's *Too Much Pressure* which was filmed at a studio in Wembley.

Above: With Dance Craze,   Bad Manners finally appeared on 2 Tone

The film perfectly captured the spirit of the bands' live performances. Up and down the country, kids abandoned their seats to dance along to the songs, filling the aisles and the pit down by the screen - much to the annoyance of the countless jobsworths who find employment at our nation's cinemas. But six of the best dance bands in the country for the price of a cinema ticket was even enough to get some Mums and Dads up on their feet (much to the embarrassment of their kids who were already dying a slow and painful death because of their parents' mere attendance). But in many ways, *Dance Craze* represented ska's last stand and it wasn't the box office smash it could have been. A year earlier and it would have been packing them in for weeks on end. In 1988, *Dance Craze* was finally made available on video (Chrysalis CVHS 5022) so those who missed the cinema showing can now sit back with a four pack, break open the popcorn and welcome the bands into their front room for a party.

A live album featuring the pick of the tracks was released simultaneously and made it to number five in the national charts. The inclusion of the two Bad Manners' tracks, *Lip Up Fatty* and *Inner London Violence*, saw the fat man and his band appear on 2 Tone after all.

Apart from *Dance Craze*, the only vinyl release from 2 Tone before the summer of '81 was Rico's *That Man Is Forward* album (2 Tone CHR TT 5005). Rico returned to Jamaica to record the LP and was joined at the Joe Gibbs Studio in Kingston by the cream of Jamaican musical talent from the past and present. Near legends like Ansell Collins, Cedric Brookes and Jah Jerry worked alongside young pretenders like Sly Dunbar and Robbie Shakespeare who were making quite a name for themselves by working with the likes of Grace Jones and in their own right.

The album's instrumental nature meant that it was never really destined to be a big commercial success, but it was very well received and fostered a cult following for Rico. It covered the entire spectrum of the man's long and varied career and was another feather in the 2 Tone cap.

The long hot summer of 1981 was one of two totally different worlds. On one hand you had the glamour and splendour of the royal wedding between the heir to the throne, Prince Charles, and his bride, Lady Diana Spencer. And on the other, you had the deprived inner-city areas of Toxteth, Brixton and Moss Side boiling over into some of the worst riots this country has seen. Watching it all on television was like taking part in the remake of *Quatermass*. The contradictions of a so-called modern society were summed up by the television newsreader who one minute told you that the bride's head-dress alone had cost £20,000, and in the next said that unemployment figures had reached an all-time high. The only thing to put a smile on your face was the helicopter filming the royal wedding procession, flying over a multi-storey car park which had ALL THE BEST TO CHAS AND DI FROM WEST HAM SKINS painted in massive letters on its roof.

If you were looking for the nation's choice of a song to sum up the troubled summer you needed to look no further than the top of the British charts. The Specials had chalked up their second number one with their new single, *Ghost Town* (2 Tone CHS TT 17). The B side featured two tracks. *Why?* was Lynval Golding's answer to those who had attacked him outside the Moonlight Club, and *Friday Night, Saturday Morning* was Terry Hall's piss-take of the disco set in much the same vein as *Stereotype*. Despite little initial airplay, the single raced up the charts and became the best ever selling single on 2 Tone, selling over a million copies. It's eerie message of violence and hopelessness was perhaps The Specials' finest three minutes and was destined to become the anthem for the troubled summer of '81.

One reason for the success of *Ghost Town* was the video that accompanied it. Videos were becoming all-important in the bid for television exposure and nobody had mastered the art better than their old friends, Madness. The nutty boys produced inventive videos one after the other that had you clamouring for more, but with *Ghost Town*, The Specials had finally given them a run for their money. The band dressed up as gangsters and raced about in cars, shooting it out in the deserted night-time streets. At one point, a £2,000 camera fell from a car, but the effect was so spectacular that it was kept in the final video.

A few English dates were played with Night Doctor in tow and then it was back to America for the band's second tour. Before crossing the Atlantic, The Specials had been due to play Dublin's Dalymount Park, but the fair city was never the luckiest of places for the band. Their visit earlier in the year had resulted in all their takings being confiscated and that little matter was still to be resolved. But even worse was the trouble that had erupted at one of the band's Dublin gigs.

"We played The Stardust Ballroom and there were no risers for the drum kit so we couldn't allow the kids on stage because it was too danngerous", said Dammers. "Then the audience started saying that we let the English kids on stage and we wouldn't let the Irish kids. And they started fighting with the bouncers. That was horrific. The bouncers had these rubber hoses filled with lead shot, that was the worst night of my life. The place burned down a week after that."

The threat of arrest over the money haul led to Dalymount Park being cancelled. Nobody could guarantee that the band wouldn't be arrested, but it was unlikely (after all they could have been arrested when the offence was committed). The promoter, Pat Egan, certainly didn't believe that was the real reason for the gig being cancelled. He sued the band for the £8,000 it had cost him to hire the football stadium. He had agreed to pay The Specials £9,000 to play the gig, but felt that the success of *Ghost Town* had led to better offers coming in. Others blamed differences within the band for the gig's cancellation, but whatever the real reason or reasons, it wasn't to be.

Above: A ticket for the gig at Dalymount Park, Dublin, that was never to be

An American tour had in fact been planned for the start of the year, but was cancelled at the last moment by Jerry. The strain of the last two years and the pressures of getting *Dance Craze* out brought him close to a nervous breakdown and a tour of Uncle Sam's would have pushed him over the brink. The tour was not as bad as the first one, but it was still demoralising and exhausting and once again the band were glad to see it finish.

On their return, everyone went back to doing their own thing, but that wasn't enough for three members of the band. Rumours started talking of a Specials split and at the start of October the rumours became a startling reality. Terry Hall, Lynval Golding and Neville Staples were leaving The Specials to form their own band, The Fun Boy Three.

At the time, Jerry, Brad and Horace were on tour with Rico and the news came like a bolt out of the blue. With perhaps the understatement of the year, Brad came out with the classic one-liner, "The band has always been pretty loose", but that didn't hide his obvious disappointment.

He was shocked and surprised by the departure of the three frontmen and also by the way it was done. It wasn't news to him that they had been working on a project together. Everyone in the band had been pushing their thumb into one pie or another, but always with the intention of returning to The Specials mother-ship. What hurt the most was the plotting and planning that must have been going on before the split and which must have included the band's manager, Rick Rogers, and engineer, Dave Jordan, because both left immediately to work with The Funboy Three. The Funboy's first single, *The Lunatics (Have Taken Over The Asylum)* on Chrysalis, was in the shops just two weeks after the formation of the new band was announced.

Dammers had little to say. "I'm disappointed, but I'm glad they stayed in the band long enough to record *Ghost Town*."

He couldn't believe that they would want to leave The Specials, particularly after the success of *Ghost Town*. The band was in such a privileged position and still had so much to achieve, and now it was all gone. For Jerry, it wasn't so much a split as a carve-up and he blamed the management for that. The endless touring routine was down to them and it was at the bottom of most of the band's troubles. The management knew that he didn't want to work with them any more and so it was little surprise to see them leave with The Funboy Three.

Above: The Specials for the last time
(Source unknown)

Even if Jerry didn't want to talk about the split, The Funboy Three were more than happy to lap up the media interest. In fact for them there could have been no better time to leave than after a massive hit single, and looking back, it had been clear in interviews that Terry, Neville and Lynval had been hinting that they were not happy with the way things were with The Specials. The six months' virtual lay-off had led to boredom and restlessness.

"That period was supposedly six months off to write songs for a new LP", said Hall, "But the three of us didn't want to write songs. We just wanted to go into the studio and do it."

The split wasn't as amicable as it might have been, but that was because of the way that it was done and not because of a big argument. The fact that the Funboys' departure came as such a surprise to the rest of the band clearly illustrated that. And talk of a split along the art college against the rest lines was well off the mark too. Everyone in the band was quite a loner and cliques didn't really come into it.

"We always had arguments in The Specials", said Terry Hall, "But show me a group that doesn't argue. In fact the reason we were so good was because of all that tension."

"The split didn't come out of any mass fight or anything. Nothing nasty happened. I just got really bored of being part of the same organisation for two and a half years."

While The Funboys were wallowing in the success of their first Top 20 hit, Roddy Radiation left to work full-time with The Tearjerkers, leaving Jerry, Brad and Horace to pick up the pieces. For them at least, The Specials and 2 Tone were worth preserving.

IN THE STUDIO

1981 came to an end with plenty of verbal about The Fun Boy Three and hardly a word from what was left of the 2 Tone camp. Roddy Radiation didn't hang around too long after The Specials' split and was soon building himself a new career with The Tearjerkers. He had wanted to team up with his brother, Mark, for a good while and now seemed as good a time as any.

"When The Specials stopped doing live gigs, we knew they were going to split", said Roddy. "I'd been told I was going to be booted out, more or less. Jerry said he couldn't work with me in the studio anymore. I got fed up with writing songs, Jerry re-arranging them and Terry singing them. Jerry wanted to put drum machines on and things."

With The Tearjerkers, Roddy could rock around the clock and write and sing songs to his heart's content. Pete Davies, who had served with Roddy in The Wild Boys before his stint with The U.K. Subs, was also in the band and the five piece outfit was completed by Joe Hughes on bass and big Slim, one of the genuine characters from the London music scene, on keyboards and accordion. After his break with The Specials, Roddy ironically got on better with Jerry than ever before and counted Lynval as one of his closest friends. For The Tearjerkers, it was back to square one with small time gigs, but after a few months, Chiswick snapped them up and released the single *Desire* (Roddy had approached 2 Tone, but, "Jerry just walked over to a wall and banged his head off it").

Meanwhile, Dammers pulled down the shutters at 2 Tone and headed off to Germany with John Bradbury and Horace Panter. They couldn't let a band like The Specials and everything it stood for just fade away and so they decided to carry on from *Ghost Town*. All three had been working on some new material for what would have been the band's third album and so the idea was to continue working as a rhythm section and wait for someone to turn up on vocals. Paul Hadfield, The Specials' old road manager, stepped in to fill the now vacant manager's shoes and they were back in business. Legal complications prevented them from using The Specials as a name so they simply went back to being called The Special A.K.A.

They were soon joined by Rhoda Dakar who had been guesting with The Specials after The Bodysnatchers split. With her, she brought an old Bodysnatchers' demo featuring that most harrowing of tunes, *The Boiler*. Jerry had wanted The Bodysnatchers to record it, but when they split the idea was put on ice. With The Special A.K.A. and Rhoda both at something of a loose end, it was decided to record the song and release it as a single. *The Boiler* (2 Tone CHS TT 18) was released during the first week of 1982, the same week that a judge unbelievably let a rapist off with a slap on the wrist and a fine. If nothing else, Dammers and friends still had that uncanny knack of reflecting society for the can of worms it is.

The Boiler was a song that you only needed to hear once. It wasn't disposable, just truly unforgettable. With its theme of rape and its all too real for comfort closing screams, it was also not the sort of song that was going to sit quaintly next to the ten-a-penny pop songs that filled the charts. Capital Radio played the record once and then removed it from its playlist, after the switchboards were jammed with complaints. People wanted to escape when they listened to their radio, not be confronted with the stark realities of life. Radio One banished the single to night-time airplay and had 'phone-in debates about the record and rape. "I became an expert on the subject overnight", said Rhoda after one radio appearance too many.

The Special A.K.A.'s ranks had been swollen for the single. Joining Rhoda, Jerry and Brad were ex-Bodysnatcher Nicky Summers on bass, Dick Cuthell on cornet and an old friend from Coventry, John Shipley on guitar. It was by far the hardest 2 Tone release of them all, and without radio exposure and no gigs to promote it, *The Boiler* was lucky to find its way to the outskirts of the Top 30. A follow up single, *Female Chauvinist Pig*, was planned, but never got further than the studio.

Above: Exit The Specials. Enter The Special A.K.A.
(Photo courtesy of Chrysalis Records Ltd. All rights reserved)

Horace didn't play on the single, what with Nicky Summers making a guest appearance, but he was back for The Special A.K.A.'s next outing, this time with Rico. *Jungle Music* (2 Tone CHS TT 19) could have come straight out of Walt Disney's *Jungle Book* let alone Walt Jabsco's stable (a compliment from a big fan of the film's music), and was Rico's most commercial release to date. He even put his trombone down often enough to supply the vocals. He was backed by the same people who worked in his touring band; Jerry, Brad, Dick, guitarist Anthony Wymhurst, Satch Dickson and Groco on percussion and of course Horace. Of all the 2 Tone records not to make the charts, the colourful *Jungle Music* has the right to feel most hard done by. Still, the public's loss was the true fan's gain.

Three months later in May, Rico was back with his final solo offering on 2 Tone, the album *Jama* (2 Tone CHS TT 5006). It was recorded partly in Jamaica (back at Joe Gibbs Studio) and partly at The Town House in London, and again it saw a wealth of Jamaican and British musical talent backing the trombone genius. Apart from the pleasant visit to *Easter Island* though, the album had little to recommend it to the mass market and again it ended up mainly in the hands of the dedicated fan.

Although Horace played bass on a couple of tracks, he left The Special A.K.A. two months before *Jama* was released. The parting was not on the friendliest of terms, with Dammers blaming Panter's involvement in the Exegesis cult and his attempts to get the rest of the band to join.

2 Tone's commitment to fostering new talent was finally to bear fruit in the summer of '82 with the release of The Apollinaires' *The Feeling's Gone* (2 Tone CHS TT 20).

The Apollinaires were a six piece band featuring Paul Tickle (on vocals), Kraig Thurnbar (drums and backing vocals), James Hunt (bass), Simon Kirk (percussion) and two guitar-touting brothers, Francis and Tom Brown. They had started life as The Volkeswagens, but changed to The Apollinaires when another band called The Volkeswagens signed to Rough Trade. With the change of name came a change in musical direction too, taking the band away from their Joy Division sound to something more akin to Haircut One Hundred. It seemed to work and they began to get a regular following in their native Leicester, a city that had hundreds of little bands at the time, all with about as much potential for success as the city's struggling football team.

The 2 Tone deal gave them the platform to reach a wider audience and for the occassion of the debut single they were helped out by Rhoda Dakar on backing vocals, a flute player by the name of Stephen Williams and another Leicester band, The Swinging Laurels. If any band was to put Leicester on the map, The Swinging Laurels were it. They even had a *Top Of The Pops* appearance to their credit, courtesy of providing the horn section for The Fun Boy Three's *The Telephone Always Rings* (Chrysalis).

The Apollinaires weren't a bad band. It's just that they weren't a particularly good one. Certainly the 2 Tone deal flattered them. Nobody really expected the label to release good old ska stompers any more, but The Apollinaires didn't even have the dance tag. The single picked up a limited amount of airplay because of the 2 Tone seal of approval, but the vocals were far too weak and the song just wasn't good enough to be talking about chart success.

A stronger second single, *Envy The Love* (2 Tone CHS TT 22), was released in November. The production on the single (handled by one of Brad's acquaintances, Warne Livesey) was a lot better and it was a good enough song if you liked that sort of thing, but again it wasn't your typical 2 Tone punter's cup of tea. It was never really going to stand out in the Christmas rush of single releases and went nowhere. The problem for The Apollinaires was that they were walking down the same funk road that had been a thriving High Street during the summer of '81, but by the end of '82 was little more than a deserted back street. Funk just wasn't selling records anymore. The band had obviously gone as far as they were ever likely to, and after the failure of the second single, the band split.

The other new 2 Tone signing of 1982, The Higsons, seemed to be trapped in a similar funk time trap.

Formed in 1980 by a group of mates from the University Of East Anglia, The Higsons had already something of a name before 2 Tone picked them up. You had a bloke going by the name of Switch on vocals, Colin Williams on bass, Stuart McGeachin and Terry Edwards both on guitar and Simon Charleton on drums. Their debut single, *I Don't Want To Live With Monkeys* on the Norwich indie label, Romans In Britain, had become a cult classic and ended up shifting over 12,000 copies. Then they released two more singles on their own Waap label, following disagreements with Romans In Britain over money.

The second of those two singles, *Conspiracy*, was released in April 1982. It had been hoped that Jerry Dammers would play keyboards on the B side, *Touchdown*, after he'd met Charleton and McGeachin at a party at Bristol. They had agreed to work together in the future, but at the time Jerry was tied up with the Rico album and trying to get The Special A.K.A. into shape and so he had to give The Higsons' single a body swerve. By the summer things were a lot quieter and Jerry agreed to produce a new song with the band in Coventry. It was called *Burn The Whole Thing Down Before The Yanks Do* and impressed Dammers enough for him to offer the band a deal with 2 Tone. It was released in October to coincide with a small U.K. tour, but not before the title was watered down to *Tear The Whole Thing Down* (2 Tone CHS TT 21).

The single was confined to a few spins on the John Peel Show and ended up in the cult file along with the band's previous offerings. A second single, *Run Me Down* (2 Tone CHS TT 24) was released in February of the following year and there was talk of an album, but the band decided to return to indie status, eventually releasing their debut *Curse Of The Higsons* LP on the Upright label. They hadn't really won many new friends or influenced too many people with the 2 Tone connection and for their troubles, they had to endure the wrath of those who clung to the idea of 2 Tone as sacred ska country. Time had ticked on, but the demise of 2 Tone and the arrival of outfits like The Apollinaires and The Higsons left a bitter taste in the mouths of those left on the once glorious 2 Tone terraces.

Above: **The Higsons**
(Picture courtesy of Chrysalis Records. All rights reserved)

Dammers was naturally disappointed with the way things had turned out for both bands. "I thought some of those records were really good. I still like *The Feeling's Gone* and *Tear The Whole Thing Down*. I don't think I did a particularly good production job on *The Feeling's Gone*. I thought it was a really good song. I still believe in that song, maybe someone should do a cover of it."

The end of 1982 saw The Special A.K.A.'s time in the studio finally being put to some use with the release of *War Crimes* (2 Tone CHS TT 23). A song about the comparisons between the Nazi atrocities in concentration camps like Bergen-Belsen, and what the Israelis were now doing to the people of Beirut, wasn't your traditional Christmas offering and received about as much airplay as a turkey sandwich gets takers on December 28th. Peel and David 'Kid' Jensen played it, but that was about your lot.

"There are certain things that radio stations feel embarrassed about playing for some reason, it's like censorship in a way", said Jerry. "I wish they'd ban our songs, but they don't - they just ignore them! The best thing that can possibly happen is to get a record into the charts and then get it banned. If you get it banned before you get into the charts however, that's a different thing altogether."

War Crimes was the first single by The Specials or The Special A.K.A. not to find its way into the charts, but it was only to be expected. A song about bombs being dropped on civilian targets and the massacre of refugees in war-torn Lebanon had to be done for its own sake, not for a quick jaunt around the *Top Of The Pops* studio. And The Special A.K.A. didn't want to make money out of children dying in hospital beds. It was enough to know that you were telling the world what was happening.

"With *The Boiler* and *War Crimes* we made those records because we felt we had to make a point, and sometimes you have to sacrifice commercial success in order to get that point across", said Dammers.

The Special A.K.A. were like The Specials growing up and venturing out into the big wide world. Instead of singing about happenings on their personal doorstep, they were now looking at wider social and political issues. And if the music business and the majority of the general public wanted to stay in the safe realms of smiling faces and bedroom posters so be it.

1983 was another quiet year for 2 Tone, with The Special A.K.A. still locked away in one studio or another working on the long-awaited album. Chrysalis were surprisingly patient with the band and were willing to stick by them, pumping some of the two million pounds profit 2 Tone had made its parent company, into studio time. When it became apparent that this wasn't going to be a cheap exercise, they moved the band to Wessex Studios which were owned by Chrysalis and didn't work out as expensive (it was costing up to £700 a day in some studios).

The Higsons' single hardly caused a ripple and it wasn't until August that The Special A.K.A. showed that rumours of their death had been greatly exaggerated with the release of the double A-sided *Racist Friend* and *Bright Lights* (2 Tone CHS TT 25).

Although both *The Boiler* and *War Crimes* were released for all the right reasons, neither did much to keep the wolves from the door. Like everyone else, The Special A.K.A. had to pay their way in the world and there was a definite attempt to make the new single more palatable. Both *Racist Friend* and *Bright Lights* were certainly more commercial, but there was to be no compromise in their lyrical content.

Racist Friend illustrated a no compromise approach to racists. If you had a racist friend (be it your brother or your sister or your mother), now was the time for that friendship to end. The basis for the song came from Jerry Dammers' recent experience of life. Once The Specials started to make it big, Jerry suddenly found himself surrounded by new 'friends'. It got to the point where the 'phone was ringing every two minutes and he was being able to devote less and less time to those who really mattered to him. In the end, he sat down with his address book and thought that scoring out anyone who was a racist would be a good start to make in

getting rid of the hangers-on.

"From my point of view, it is not enough to just be anti-racist yourself", explained Jerry. "You have to be a positive anti-racist. You have to make a stand against it, because otherwise nothing ever changes."

Bright Lights illustrated the realities behind the streets paved with gold myth that has hundreds of young people heading for London every year. Life was not one big party as portrayed by the bands of the moment, Wham!, Duran Duran and Spandau Ballet. It might have been okay for them to live in a pop dream world, but it wasn't for The Special A.K.A. And it wasn't jealousy on the band's part either. It was just difficult to hide behind jolly pop songs when kids leaving school were working for the government signing dole cheques.

The single got to number 60 in the charts, but failed to get the airplay needed to take it higher. By now, The Special A.K.A. was working as a pool of musicians with others being drafted in as and when needed. There was of course Jerry, Brad and Rhoda, and they were joined by John Shipley on his guitar, a vocalist by the name of Stan Campbell and Gary McManus on bass to form the core of the outfit.

Stan came from Coventry and met Jerry in a cafe after a friend had pointed him out as a Grace Jones look-a-like. Gary went to Warwick University and before stepping into The Special A.K.A. frame, played bass with local band, The Defendants. Horace Panter was still in the game for *War Crimes*, but by *Racist Friend*, Gary had replaced him in the band.

On the fringes of the band were people like Egidio Newton, a friend of Rhoda's (they had met outside David Bowie's house when they were both big fans of the man) who had been in a number of London bands, including the soul funk Animal Nightlife, and violinist, Nick Parker, who added to the eery feel of *War Crimes*. Dick Cuthell was always on hand when needed and for *Racist Friend*, Roddy Radiation made a welcome return.

The idea was to function as a fluid affair, where members could come and go. It was very rare for everyone to be in the studio at the same time, not least because half the band lived in Coventry and the rest in London, and this added to the delays of getting both the band and album together. 1983 turned into 1984 and The Special A.K.A. had still never appeared live and had only three minor hits to their credit. In a bid to get some money rolling in, Chrysalis released the compilation album, *This Are 2 Tone* (2 Tone CHR TT 5007) which featured previously released tracks from the 2 Tone singles vault. Launched on to the Christmas market, it was received as a sort of novelty *Greatest Hits* item and bought by those who had missed all the good old days, but wanted it for their Christmas party. It reached number 51 and that was about its lot. It was almost as if it heralded the end of 2 Tone, but anyone writing off the label or The Special A.K.A. was about to eat his or her hat. *Lonely Crowd* was expected to be the next single, but instead *Nelson Mandela* (2 Tone CHS TT 26) was chosen to lead the band back to the charts.

Nelson Mandela was one of the jailed leaders of the banned African National Congress, a movement established to fight South Africa's apartheid political system. A lawyer by profession, Mandela helped set up the A.N.C.'s youth wing in 1944 and five years later was elected to the Congress' ruling body. Tired of waiting for political change while black people lived in squalor, he went underground to form the organisation's armed wing, Umkhonto We Sizwe (Spear Of The Nation) and became a top target for the South African government. He went into hiding after receiving guerilla training in Algeria, but managed to leave the country to visit London. He was captured soon after his return to South Africa and in 1962 was sentenced to five years imprisonment for organising protests against the constitution.

In '63, while serving that sentence, he was put back on trial and charged with sabotage and attempting to cause violent revolution. He was found guilty and sentenced to life imprisonment with little real hope of ever being released. The publicity surrounding the trial won him a place in the hearts of millions of black South Africans and Mandela became a symbol of the fight against apartheid.

Jerry Dammers didn't really know a great deal about the plight of South Africa until he attended Mandela's 60th Birthday Party at Alexandra Palace in London. It was organised by the Anti-Apartheid Movement and Jerry became increasingly involved in its work, eventually helping to form the Artists Against Apartheid offshoot.

The single, *Nelson Mandela*, saw something akin to the gathering of the clans and was recorded in just four days (quite an achievement for The Special A.K.A.). Dick Cuthell was back on trumpet and three new faces, Andy Aderinto, David Heath and Paul Speare, chipped in on saxaphone, flute and penny whistle respectively. Backing vocals were provided by Lynval Golding (who was now a free agent after The Funboys had split), ex-Beat boys Ranking Roger and Dave Wakeling (now working together in General Public), Molly and Polly Jackson, the three girl band Afrodiziak, and Elvis Costello, who was also behind the mixing desks for the first time for 2 Tone since *Specials* in '79.

"I think it was good to have an outsider, because I'd been producing everything", said Dammers who was always too much the perfectionist. "And it was getting very bogged down, so it was like a fresh pair of ears."

Although it was a plea for the release of Nelson Mandela, who was 65 at the time, the song had a very powerful air of celebration about it. One that was to guarantee radio play and see *Nelson Mandela* climb to number nine in the charts. For Dammers and everyone involved, it was a triumph. Not only was The Special A.K.A. in the Top Ten, but it was achieved with a serious message. According to Jerry, "Pop is giving people what they want to hear. We're giving people what they don't want to hear", but for once the general public did want to hear all about Nelson Mandela.

It was illegal to even have a picture of Nelson Mandela in South Africa and the record was instantly banned (government controlled newspapers there claimed that the single had flopped in the U.K.). People were jailed for wearing Nelson Mandela t-shirts so they were unlikely to be rushing into record shops to by the single anyway. Chrysalis South Africa sent a rushed telex to London, telling Chrysalis U.K. not to send over any copies of the single for fear of prosecution. But the song and the message got through. No doubt one of Dammers' proudest moments would have been seeing ITV's *News At Ten* broadcasting pictures of a rally in South Africa, with the largely black crowd singing the words to *Nelson Mandela*.

With The Special A.K.A.'s aversion to gigs, it was left to African Connection to play *Nelson Mandela* to the crowd of 20,000 people in London's Jubilee Gardens to celebrate 25 years of the Anti-Apartheid Movement in August, 1984. But in 1988, Dammers was joined on stage by a host of musicians to play the song at the huge Nelson Mandela Birthday Concert at Wembley Stadium. Big names like Stevie Wonder, Simple Minds and The Eurythmics lended their support to the biggest musical happening since Live Aid; but like Live Aid, it was one of those events where money (twenty five notes), and not commitment, got you in the door.

To coincide with the Wembley event, Chrysalis released a sluggish re-mix of the song called *Free Nelson Mandela* with Ndonda Khuze on lead vocals, Jonas Gwangwa on trombone and scratching by Chris Long (The Rhythm Doctor). Although released with the blessing of 2 Tone, the single was a straight Chrysalis issue and not on the chequered label.

Nelson Mandela was finally released from captivity in February 1990, and as crowds gathered outside the South African Embassy in Trafalgar Square, the words to *Nelson Mandela* once again filled the air. It might not have topped the charts like *Too Much Too Young* or *Ghost Town*, but *Nelson Mandela* will be the one remembered long after any of the 2 Tone releases have gone to the heaven for forgotten hits.

The success of the single boded well for the album which finally saw the light of day in August 1984. It had taken three years in the making and had cost a rumoured £500,000 plus to complete, making it the most expensive album ever at the time. The delay in its release had Jerry talking about re-drawing Walt Jabsco in a bathchair covered in cobwebs.

"What people have to remember is that the first Specials' LP took two years before that came out", explained Jerry. "This band is a completely different band, and we're really just at the stage of the first Specials' LP. It's hard because you just can't go down the local pub and do gigs and develop naturally because there's so much attention."

The Special A.K.A. had got off on the wrong foot from day one, and although hiding away in a studio seemed like a good idea at the time, it turned out to be a very costly mistake. The plan should have been to get the band on the road, release a few singles and then see about an album based on the band's live set. Instead, Jerry put his head down and blundered his way through in a doomed attempt to fulfill the contractual agreement that demanded five albums from him. Still its easy to be wise after the event, but even after a few months the album could have been scrapped and wasn't, because Jerry was determined to see it through to the bitter end.

Media attention had something to do with the failure of The Special A.K.A. to take to the stage, but it wasn't the complete story. A few photographers down the front at gigs and the odd interview would hardly have been a major problem for what was after all a collection of mostly experienced musicians. A fear of failure was probably closer to the mark, a fear reinforced time and time again as the months of studio life ticked by. What was also true was that The Special A.K.A. were almost a band by name only. Even in the studio, they were hardly ever together. Rhoda only ever met Stan Campbell a couple of times, despite sharing the vocal duties with him. The Specials were always a live experience, with Jerry Dammers even going as far as saying that records were a waste of time. With The Special A.K.A. he couldn't have got much further from his original ideals and was the first to admit it. For someone who had always claimed to hate studios, The Special A.K.A. and its music were very much his studio creations.

To be fair, gigging wasn't as easy as jumping in a van and setting up stall. Most of the songs had been written with The Specials in mind, and it did take time to adapt the talents of a new band to them. What's more, Jerry was determined to make the band as democratic as possible. Part of the reason for The Specials splitting was the fact that Jerry got most of the attention and was seen as something of a dictator within the band. He didn't want the same to happen again, but inevitably joint decisions took a lot longer to reach than a single person's. Watch the pennies and the pounds will take care of themselves took on a whole new meaning, as everybody's two pennies' worth ran up a bill of half a million pounds.

Another reason for not gigging was Stan Campbell's decision to quit the band to pursue a solo career with WEA, just before the album was released. He was first and foremost a soul singer, and it wasn't easy adapting songs to suit his voice. When things went wrong in the studio, rather than buckle under, Stan made almost daily threats to leave which certainly didn't help matters.

When the album was released the only title for it was *In The Studio* (2 Tone CHR TT 5008). That's where The Special A.K.A. had spent the last three years with Jerry often hanging around after everyone else had gone home to tinker about with the sound of this and that.

The studio doors were flung open and the public allowed in to sample the band's wares, but there were few surprises. Four of the ten tracks had already appeared in single format and a fifth, *Girlfriend*, was about to join them. Despite being recorded over such a lengthy period and despite the varied mix of soul, reggae, jazz and funk, the album sounded remarkably intact. It might not have been as instantly contagious as *Specials*, but there was no doubting the quality of *In The Studio* or its ability to grow on you.

Described by Dammers as an album warning against excesses, it touched on problems both personal and global. *Nelson Mandela* and *War Crimes* were both there, drawing people's attention away from their own little worlds to events happening thousands of miles away. Closer to home, there were tracks like *Alcohol*, reflecting Dammers joining the wagon after being a bottle of whisky a day man, and *Housebound*, a poke at Terry Hall who rarely ventured outside his front door in case he was recognised. *Lonely Crowd* showed the loneliness behind the false smiles at nightclubs, where a lot of very unhappy people go through the motions of pretending their having the time of their lives. The second verse of *Lonely Crowd* focused on the knife attack on Lynval Golding at a Coventry nightclub which left him hospitalised with 31 stitches in his face and neck (The Funboy Three had to postpone their first U.K. tour because of Lynval's condition, but he made a remarkable recovery and was never bitter about the attack).

Dammers was pleased with the album. Pleased with the results and pleased to have 2 Tone's answer to painting the Forth Bridge off his shoulders.

"This LP's a once in a lifetime thing," he said. "I love messing around in the studio, but unless I build my own, I'll never get the chance to do it again. I can't afford it."

Even with the album to promote, Dammers still didn't take the band on the road. In an apparent bid to avoid contact with the public that would have put a smile on Howard Hughes' face, The Special A.K.A. poured all their efforts into television and video instead. In September, the band were featured in a one hour documentary for Channel 4's *Play At Home* series, which saw the band rehearsing, talking about their music and generally going about their lives. They also made a late night appearing on *Switch*, but the only other way of seeing the band was on the video, *On Film* (Palace Videos in conjunction with Chrysalis CVIM 15).

On Film was released as a substitute to live performances and featured all of the songs from the album, bar *Night On The Tiles*. Some of the tracks were taken from *Play At Home* and the others were promotional videos made for single releases. Although low budget (Dammers liked to see them as B movies), there are some great moments on it. It's worth buying just to see Dick Cuthell's ridiculous moustache and Jerry in a space-suit and a pair of Stanley Matthews shorts. Violinist Nick Parker didn't appear in the *War Crimes* video, his place being taken by one John Taylor.

TAKEN FROM "IN THE STUDIO"
"THE BEST LONG PLAYER THIS YEAR"
Record Mirror

THE SPECIAL AKA
"WHAT I LIKE MOST ABOUT YOU IS YOUR GIRLFRIEND!"

NEW 12 + 7 INCH SINGLE

c/w
"CAN'T GET A BREAK"
(PREVIOUSLY UNRELEASED TRACK)

12" EXTENDED VERSION INCLUDES FREE POSTER. LIMITED EDITION 7" VERSION AVAILABLE IN A GATEFOLD SLEEVE

MARKETED BY CHRYSALIS RECORDS

One of the best videos is for *Girlfriend*, a song released as a single in August as *What I Like Most About You Is Your Girlfriend* (2 Tone CHS TT 27) with the previously unreleased *Can't Get A Break*. Despite being released in every format known to marketing man, the single struggled into the lower reaches of the charts, refusing to go higher than number 51. *In The Studio* had made its way to number 36 in the album charts, but was not the success that either Chrysalis or The Special A.K.A. had hoped for. No doubt the lack of gigs and abundance of singles had a lot to answer for on that score.

Another single, *You Can't Take Love Seriously*, was planned, but by then 2 Tone had run out of money and Chrysalis had run out of patience. The contract said three albums, but *In The Studio* had eaten the budget for them all and hadn't exactly gone out of its way to repay it. He couldn't make any more records, but at the same time Chrysalis were not going to let him go as easily as that. Not after forking out all that money for the album anyway.

"The record company has computers and they ask the computer, 'How much money will Jerry Dammers make?', explained Jerry. "And the computer says, 'Nothing'. But I can't see how a computer can forecast what kind of music I'm going to make. It's ridiculous."

So the final word from The Special A.K.A. was *What I Like Most About You Is Your Girlfriend*. They set off in the direction of a new singer and were never to be seen again.

GHOST TOWN

Jerry Dammers might have been broke and in debt to Chrysalis, but he could still hold his head up high. In a crooked game, he'd played an honest hand and come up trumps with both 2 Tone and The Specials. And the lack of money and backing didn't stop Dammers throwing everything he had into the *Starvation* charity project at the start of 1985. Ethiopia was once against suffering at the hands of famine and war, and thousands were starving to death. Band Aid's *Do They Know It's Christmas Time?/Feed The World* had dominated the press and charts at the end of 1984, and 1985 was to be the year that the pop world pricked a nation's conscience into giving millions more to ease the suffering with Live Aid.

The idea for *Starvation* actually came before Bob Geldof had assembled Band Aid, but whereas *Do They Know It's Christmas Time?/Save The World* was recorded and in the shops within days, *Starvation* took months to see through to the finish.

It all started when a young Madness fan strolled into the Zarjazz office and suggested that Madness recorded The Pioneers 1970 hit, *Starvation*. The project blossomed and into Madness' Liquidator Studios trooped members of UB40, Madness, The Specials, General Public and The Pioneers to name just a few, to record their version of *Starvation*, described by Pioneer Jackie Robinson as "better than the original". All of the proceeds from band royalties went to charities working in Ethiopia, Eritrea and Sudan, and although completely overshadowed by the publicity surrounding Band Aid, the gesture was appreciated and rewarded with a number 33 chart place.

This little gathering brought back memories of 2 Tone's wonderful past, but there was still life in the old dog yet. Over a year was allowed to pass before 2 Tone once again ventured into the outside world with a single from new blood, The Friday Club, a seven piece outfit from Scarborough.

With The Friday Club came a blend of soul and jazz funk that was to hold them in good stead in the clubs. Theirs was a world of northern soul and although far from a mere copy of Wigan Casino's heroes, it was obvious where the band found their inspiration. The band used the sound of soul to carry social and political messages similar to those of The Special A.K.A., but the music was just a little too bland to get them across effectively. Despite the obvious talents of singer-songwriter Andrew Brooks and the brilliant voice of Terri Bateman who also played sax, The Friday Club lacked that killer punch and The Redskins they were not.

Above: **The Friday Club**
(Photo courtesy of Chrysalis Records Ltd. All rights reserved)

Throughout 1985, the band had worked hard at building a following in the trendier nightclubs and had done well for themselves. July saw them play at the Alternative Top Of The Pops gig in London where record companies were asked to come and view the future of rock n' roll. Joining The Friday Club in the starting blocks were other bands hoping to be discovered like Hipsway, The Pet Shop Boys and Curiosity Killed The Cat. September saw them play the Rock For Jobs gig at Liverpool's Sefton Park with The Redskins and comedian Alexei Sayle and soon afterwards the single deal with 2 Tone was struck.

The single, *Window Shopping* (2 Tone CHS TT 28) was released at the end of October and was given the best possible boost when The Friday Club were announced as the support band on Madness' Mad Not Mad Tour. Madness had not toured the U.K. since the start of 1983, but the month long tour soon saw the band re-establish themselves as one of the best live bands in the business. Sadly, the tour did little for The Friday Club. The single disappeared without a trace as did the band soon afterwards.

Perhaps Dammers could have opened a few more publicity doors for the band. The song was never a chart topper, but it was pleasant enough to pathe the way for future success. But by October, Jerry was too involved in another musical project, this time to promote the cause of Namibian independence from South Africa. He produced and arranged *The Wind Of Change* (Rough Trade) for Robert Wyatt & The SWAPO Singers, which also boasted the involvement of Lynval Golding and Dick Cuthall. And then along came Billy Bragg with Red Wedge and Jerry was off again on a political crusade against the Tories.

Apart from Jerry, only John Bradbury remained on board the floating museum that 2 Tone had so quickly become. Madness, The Beat and even The Specials seemed remarkably dated less than ten years on. It was quite fitting though that the final salvo fired from her decks was a single from Brad's band, J.B.'s All Stars. He had formed the band as a soul revue in 1983 with Dee Sharp on vocals and percussion, Mark Hughes on harmonica, Jason Votier on trumpet and flugel horn, Robert Awahi on rhythm guitar, Steve Nieve on piano and string synthesiser and George Webley on bass.

Prior to the 2 Tone release of January 1986, J.B.'s All Stars had in fact secured a deal with RCA, which had resulted in the three singles, *One Minute Every Hour*, *Sign On The Dotted Line* and *Ready Willing And Able*. The teachers' strike provided the backdrop to *Alphabet Army* (2 Tone CHS TT 29) - "If you can read this, thank a teacher", ran the ads for the single - but it received minimal airplay and fell well short of a chart place.

2 Tone was still producing highly relevant music, but in a get-rich-quick society of I'm Alright Jacks nobody seemed to be listening anymore. The 2 Tone flame that had burnt so brightly during the glorious summer of '79 could hardly light a cigarette with its final offering, but that wasn't as important as trying to get the message across. Everything you touch won't turn to gold, but at least 2 Tone's heart remained in the right place. And there can be no doubt that it was a heart made of pure gold.

YOU'RE WONDERING NOW

Above: **Jerry Dammers**
(Photo courtesy of Chrysalis Records Ltd. All rights reserved)

After *Alphabet Army*, Chrysalis closed the lid on the 2 Tone box, but kept hold of the key. The 29 singles and eight albums were put into safe-keeping until the tenth anniversary of *Gangsters* reaching the charts. Then Chrysalis invited Dammers to select his favourite tracks for the release of a double album, *The Two Tone Story* (2 Tone CHR TT 5009). It walked much the same path as *This Are 2 Tone* and *Dance Craze* with its mix of studio and live cuts, and the only previously unreleased track on it was a live version of *Stereotype*. It would have been nice to see a side devoted to 2 Tone rarities like *Raquel*, a Specials' song released on the

B side of a live *Concrete Jungle*, but only in Holland, and on an *NME* cassette.

It was released after fans had written in to Chrysalis asking for the anniversary to be marked and amidst talk of an imminent ska revival centred around a whole new host of bands from all over the world. *The Two Tone Story* was no doubt a chance to chip away at the debts from The Special A.K.A.'s album, but money wasn't the only motive. The double album package was actually sold into shops for the price of a single LP, although the gatefold sleeve saw the larger chains banging out copies at the full double album price.

Despite the press coverage and the posters plastered around the town, it just wasn't the same. Listening to *Gangsters* in a trendy club sandwiched between Bros and The Beastie Boys makes you want to stop the world for a moment. Hold on there! 2 Tone's trying to tell you something and all you can do is dance away to anything the DJ plays to you. Still, for most people music is as disposable as an empty crisp packet.

Long gone are the days when you were messing about in the queue to see the best in live band entertainment. Long gone are the days when the ritual of having your hair cropped and pulling on a pair of Doc Marten's made you feel ten feet tall when you were really four feet nothing. Gone too are the days when you'd return to your classroom to find your 2 Tone clad text books covered in "Mod bastard!" graffitti thanks to some hairy dinosaur.

Today 2 Tone is seen as just another small piece in the music jigsaw puzzle and all you get is a load of bollocks about, "But did 2 Tone ever achieve anything?"

Did The Beatles ever achieve anything? Did Pink Floyd? The Sex Pistols or The Bay City Rollers? Dammers wasn't running for Prime Minister for God's sake. He was running a record label that mixed politics and music without having to resort to Sixth Form rhetoric. The no future brigade of '76 with their safety pins and swastikas didn't have it as hard as the class of '79 in terms of unemployment and prospects, but if you want to know what 2 Tone achieved you can have it in a word. Inspiration. The 2 Tone message said you don't have to take any of this. It said, get up off your arse and do something for yourself. Stand up and do your own thing.

2 Tone came along to tell us that we weren't the same as those who had it all. We were better and they'd better start to believe it too! A simple old record label gave thousands of kids a sense of identity, loyalty and pride. If you could live through 2 Tone and still ask if it achieved anything, you were walking a different street to me.

This were 2 Tone.

DISCOGRAPHY

The SPECIAL A.K.A.
Gangsters
TT1/TT2

ELVIS COSTELLO & THE ATTRACTIONS
I Can't Stand Up For Falling Down
CHS TT 7

THE SPECIAL A.K.A.
Too Much Too Young (Live EP)
CHS TT 7

THE SELECTER
Nissing Words (miss-press)
CHS TT 10

THE SPECIALS
Do Nothing
CHS TT 16

THE SPECIALS
Ghost Town
CHS TT 17

DISCOGRAPHY

What follows is a complete British 2 Tone discography. Most of the records below are available on foreign release, often in very attractive and different picture sleeves. Other known releases are at the end of this discography in the Rarities section.

7" SINGLES

TT 1/TT 2   THE SPECIALS - *Gangsters* / THE SELECTER - *Selecter*

CHS TT 3   MADNESS - *The Prince* / *Madness*

CHS TT 4   THE SELECTER - *On My Radio* / *Too Much Pressure*

CHS TT 5   THE SPECIALS - *A Message To You Rudy* / *Nite Klub*

CHS TT 6   THE BEAT - *Tears Of A Clown* / *Ranking Full Stop*

CHS TT 7   ELVIS COSTELLO & THE ATTRACTIONS - *I Can't Stand Up For Falling Down* / *Girls Talk*[1]

CHS TT 7   THE SPECIAL A.K.A. - *Too Much Too Young* and *Guns Of Navarone* / *Skinhead Symphony: Longshot Kick The Bucket, Liquidator* and *Skinhead Moonstomp* (live EP)

CHS TT 8   THE SELECTER - *Three Minute Hero* / *James Bond*

CHS TT 9   THE BODYSNATCHERS - *Let's Do Rock Steady* / *Ruder Than You*

CHS TT 10   THE SELECTER - *Missing Words* / *Carry Go Bring Come* (live)

CHS TT 11   THE SPECIALS - *Rat Race* / *Rude Buoys Outa Jail*

CHS TT 12   THE BODYSNATCHERS - *Easy Life* / *Too Experienced*

CHS TT 13   THE SPECIALS - *Stereotype* / *International Jetset*

CHS TT 14   THE SWINGING CATS - *Away* / *Mantovani*

CHS TT 15   RICO - *Sea Cruise* / *Carolina*

CHS TT 16   THE SPECIALS - *Do Nothing* / *Maggie's Farm*[2]

CHS TT 17   THE SPECIALS - *Ghost Town* / *Why?* and *Friday Night Saturday Morning*

RHODA WITH THE SPECIAL A.K.A.
The Boiler
CHS TT 18

RICO AND THE SPECIAL A.K.A.
Jungle Music
CHS TT 19

THE APOLLINAIRES
The Feeling's Gone
CHS TT 20

THE HIGSONS
Tear The Whole Thing Down
CHS TT 21

THE APOLLINAIRES
Envy The Love
CHS TT 22

THE SPECIAL A.K.A.
War Crimes
CHS TT 23

CHS TT 18   RHODA WITH THE SPECIAL A.K.A. - *The Boiler / Theme From The Boiler*[3]

CHS TT 19   RICO AND THE SPECIAL A.K.A.   - *Jungle Music / Rasta Call You*

CHS TT 20   THE APOLLINAIRES - *The Feeling's Gone / The Feeling's Back*

CHS TT 21   THE HIGSONS - *Tear The Whole Thing Down / Ylang Ylang*

CHS TT 22   THE APOLLINAIRES   - *Envy The Love / Give It Up*

CHS TT 23   THE SPECIAL A.K.A. - *War Crimes (The Crime Remains The Same) / Version*

CHS TT 24   THE HIGSONS - *Run Me Down / Put The Punk Back Into Funk*

CHS TT 25   THE SPECIAL A.K.A. - *Racist Friend / Bright Lights*[4]

CHS TT 26   THE SPECIAL A.K.A. - *Nelson Mandela / Break Down The Door*

CHS TT 27   THE SPECIAL A.K.A. - *What I Like Most About You Is Your Girlfriend / Can't Get A Break*[5]

CHS TT 28   THE FRIDAY CLUB - *Window Shopping / Window Shopping (Instrumental)*

CHS TT 29   J.B.'S ALLSTARS - *The Alphabet Army / Al. Arm*

[1] As stated in the main text, this Costello single was withdrawn because of the threat of legal action and the 13,000 copies pressed were mostly given away free at Costello gigs. Today, it commands anything up to £20 (1990) in collector's shop and is probably the most sought after 2 Tone release.

[2] Prior to the release of *Do Nothing*, only the *Too Much Too Young* live EP had appeared in a picture sleeve. From here onwards, all of the 2 Tone singles are available in picture sleeve.

[3] *The Boiler* was the last 2 Tone single to be released with the famous 2 Tone paper label centre. Usually the first pressing was released with a paper label and the rest plastic silver centres (except *Nelson Mandela* which was available firstly with a gold plastic centre and then with a silver centre).

[4] *Racist Friend* was available in picture disc format too (CHS TPTT 25).

[5] *What I Like Most About You Is Your Girlfriend* was also available in picture disc format

THE HIGSONS
Run Me Down
CHS TT 24

THE SPECIAL A.K.A.
Racist Friend
CHS TT 25

THE SPECIAL A.K.A.
Nelson Mandela
CHS TT 26

THE SPECIAL A.K.A.
What I Like Most About You Is Your Girlfriend
CHS TT 27

THE FRIDAY CLUB
Window Shopping
CHS TT 28

J.B.'S ALL STARS
The Alphabet Army
CHS TT 29

(CHS TPTT 27). Chrysalis really went to town with this one, releasing it in a gatefold sleeve too (the first copies of which contained a free copy of the *War Crimes* single).

10" SINGLES

CHS TT 1023   THE SPECIAL A.K.A - *War Crimes (The Crime Remains The Same) / Version*

12" SINGLES

CHS TT 1217   THE SPECIALS - *Ghost Town / Why?* and *Friday Night Saturday Morning*

CHS TT 1218   RHODA WITH THE SPECIAL A.K.A. - *The Boiler / Theme From The Boiler*

CHS TT 1219   RICO AND THE SPECIAL A.K.A. - *Jungle Music / Rasta Call You* and *Easter Island*

CHS TT 1220   THE APOLLINAIRES - *The Feeling's Gone (Dance Mix) / The Feeling's Back* and *The Bongo Medley*

CHS TT 1221   THE HIGSONS - *Tear The Whole Thing Down / Ylang Ylang*

CHS TT 1222   THE APOLLINAIRES - *Envy The Love / Give It Up*

CHS TT 1224   THE HIGSONS - *Run Me Down / Put The Punk Back Into Funk*

CHS TT 1225   THE SPECIAL A.K.A. - *Racist Friend* and *Bright Lights / Racist Friend (instrumental)* and *Bright Lights (instrumental)*

CHS TT 1226   THE SPECIAL A.K.A. - *Nelson Mandela / Break Down The Door*

CHS TT 1227   THE SPECIAL A.K.A. - *What I Like Most About You Is Your Girlfriend / Can't Get A Break*[6]

CHS TT 1228   THE FRIDAY CLUB - *Window Shopping / Window Shopping (Instrumental)*

THE SPECIALS
Specials
CDL TT 5001

THE SELECTER
Too Much Pressure
CDL TT 5002

THE SPECIALS
More Specials
CHR TT 5003

VARIOUS
Dance Craze
CHR TT 5004

RICO
This Man Is Forward
CHR TT 5005

RICO
Jama
CHR TT 5006

CHS TT 1229 J.B.'S ALLSTARS - *The Alphabet Army / The Alphabet Army and Al. Arm*

[6] This 12" single came with a free poster of the sleeve. I'm not really one to talk because I'd pay good money for a paper bag if it had 2 Tone written on it, but the truth is that for the most part, 2 Tone 12" releases offered nothing different to the 7" releases and so represented very poor value for money.

ALBUMS

CDL TT 5001 THE SPECIALS - *Specials*

A Message To You Rudy, Do The Dog, It's Up To You, Nite Klub, Doesn't Make It Alright, Concrete Jungle and *Too Hot / Monkey Man, (Dawning Of A) New Era, Blank Expression, Stupid Marriage, Too Much Too Young, Little Bitch* and *You're Wondering Now*[7]

CDL TT 5002 THE SELECTER - *Too Much Pressure*

Three Minute Hero, Time Hard (called *Everyday* on the actual record, but by its correct title *Time Hard* on the sleeve), *They Make Me Mad, Missing Words, Danger, Street Feeling* and *My Collie Not A Dog / Too Much Pressure, Murder, Out On The Streets, Carry Go Bring Come, Black And Blue* and *James Bond*

CHR TT 5003 THE SPECIALS - *More Specials*

Enjoy Yourself (It's Later Than You Think), Man At C&A, Hey Little Rich Girl, Do Nothing, Pearl's Cafe and *Sock It To 'Em J.B. / Stereotypes, Stereotypes (Part Two), Holiday Fortnight, I Can't Stand It, International Jetset* and *Enjoy Yourself (Reprise)*[8]

CHR TT 5004 VARIOUS - *Dance Craze*

THE SPECIALS - *Concrete Jungle*, THE BEAT - *Mirror In The Bathroom*, BAD MANNERS - *Lip Up Fatty*, THE SELECTER - *Three Minute Hero*, THE BODYSNATCHERS - *Easy Life*, THE BEAT - *Big Shot* and MADNESS - *One Step Beyond /* THE BEAT - *Ranking Full Stop*, THE

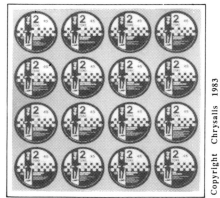

VARIOUS
This Are 2 Tone
CHR TT 5007

THE SPECIAL A.K.A.
In The Studio
CHR TT 5008

VARIOUS
The Two Tone Story
CHR TT 5009

THE SPECIALS
Concrete Jungle
Dutch import

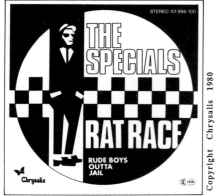

THE SPECIALS
Rat Race
German import

RODDY RADIATION & THE SPECIALS
Braggin' & Tryin' Not To Lie
TT 999

SPECIALS - *Man At C&A*, THE SELECTER - *Missing Words*, BAD MANNERS - *Inner London Violence*, MADNESS - *Night Boat To Cairo*, THE SELECTER - *Too Much Pressure* and THE SPECIALS - *Nite Klub*[9]

CHR TT 5005 RICO - *That Man Is Forward*

Easy Snappin', Fiesta, Chang Kai Shek and *Stay Out Late / Red Top, X, Ganja* and *That Man Is Forward*

CHR TT 5006 RICO - *Jama*

Destroy Them, We Want Peace, Jam Rock, Some Day and *Distant Drums / Love And Justice, Java, Do The Reload* and *Easter Island*

CHR TT 5007 VARIOUS - *This Are Two Tone*

THE SPECIAL A.K.A. - *Gangsters*, MADNESS - *Madness*, THE SELECTER - *On My Radio*, THE BEAT - *Tears Of A Clown*, THE SPECIALS - *Rudi, A Message To You*, THE SELECTER - *Too Much Pressure*, THE BODYSNATCHERS - *Too Experienced / THE BEAT - Ranking Full Stop* and THE SPECIALS - *Too Much Too Young* / THE SELECTER - *The Seleter*, THE SPECIALS - *Stereotype*, THE SWINGING CATS - *Mantovani*, RICO - *Jungle Music*, RHODA & THE SPECIAL A.K.A. - *The Boiler* and THE SPECIALS - *Ghost Town*[10]

CHR TT 5008 SPECIAL A.K.A. - *In The Studio*

Bright Lights, Lonely Crowd, Girlfriend, House Bound and *Night On The Tiles / Nelson Mandela, War Crimes, Racist Friend, Alcohol* and *Break Down The Door.*

CHR TT 5009 VARIOUS - *The 2 Tone Story* (double album)

THE SELECTER - *The Seleter*, THE SPECIAL A.K.A. - *Gangsters*, MADNESS - *The Prince*, THE SELECTER - *On My Radio*, THE SPECIALS - *Rudi, A Message To You*, THE BEAT - *Ranking Full Stop* and THE BODYSNATCHERS - *Ruder Than You* / RICO - *That Man Is Forward*, THE SPECIALS - *Blank Expression*, THE SPECIALS - *Do Nothing*, THE SPECIALS - *International Jet Set*, THE SPECIALS - *Why?*, THE SPECIALS - *Ghost Town* and RICO - *Easter Island.*

THE SELECTER - *Too Much Pressure* (live), BAD MANNERS - *Lip Up Fatty* (live), THE SPECIALS - *Stereotype* (live), THE BEAT - *Mirror In The Bathroom* (live), THE SELECTER - *Three Minute Hero* (live), THE SPECIALS - *Too Much Too Young* (live) and MADNESS - *One Step Beyond* (live) / RHODA & THE SPECIAL A.K.A. - *The Boiler*, THE SPECIAL

A.K.A. - *Racist Friend*, THE SPECIAL A.K.A. - *War Crimes*, THE SPECIAL A.K.A. - *Nelson Mandela* and RICO - *Destroy Them*.

[7] All of the albums on 2 Tone were also available in cassette format and a number are now available on compact disc (The Specials - *Specials*, The Specials - *More Specials*, Various - *This Are Two Tone* and Various - *The Two Tone Story*). The cassette version of *Specials* included an extra track, *Gangsters*, as did the American vinyl version of the album.

[8] The Specials ended up with too many tracks for *More Specials* and so put two tracks on a free single which was given away free with the first 100,000 copies of the album. It features a Roddy Radiation number called *Braggin' & Tryin' Not To Lie* and a different version of *Rude Buoys Outa Jail* by Neville Staples AKA Judge Roughneck. A free poster of the album cover also went out with the first 100,000.

[9] Again, a free poster was given away with this album. Also, chains like Virgin and HMV regularly gave away badges, ties and other posters with this and other 2 Tone albums.

[10] Yet another free poster for those who were lucky enough to be at the front of the queue. This album was also available in pink or blue.

Of the above records, only the following albums have not been deleted:

CDLTT 5001   The Selecter - *Too Much Pressure* (cassette version deleted)

CHRTT 5003   The Specials - *More Specials*

CHRTT 5004   Various - *Dance Craze*

CHRTT 5007   Various - *This Are Two Tone*

CHRTT 5008   The Special A.K.A. - *In The Studio*

CHRTT 5009   Various - *The Two Tone Story*

VARIOUS
Dance Craze (video)
Chrysalis CVHS 5022

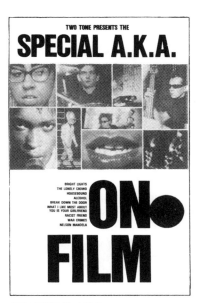

THE SPECIAL A.K.A.
On Film (video)
Chrysalis CVIM 15

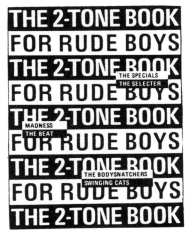

Miles
THE TWO TONE BOOK FOR RUDE BOYS
Omnibus

The two magazines published for the film Dance Craze

RARITIES, VIDEOS, BOOKS AND MAGAZINES

Record-wise, most 2 Tone releases are highly sought after, but you can still find most of them tucked away at low prices in second-hand record shops. Top of most collectors' lists are the Elvis Costello single and *Concrete Jungle* backed by *Raquel* in single format (Dutch import) plus any bootleg offerings. Since the last edition, we have been told of at least four Specials' bootleg albums alone.

The most important was the *Live In Manchester* release, which came out before The Specials' debut album. Most people got it for a fiver at the time, which meant they not only got a bargain, but could also sing along at gigs. There are other similar albums called *Live At The Moonlight Club*, *Rude Buoys Outa Jail* and *Live In Hamburg*. There is also a *Live At The Lyceum* album in a great sleeve and with great sound quality, but word has it that this wasn't a bootleg at all, but a promo release for French radio.

Singles by the lesser known 2 Tone bands are also becoming harder to find as are imports, some of which feature tracks that didn't appear in 7" in the U.K.

There are three 2 Tone videos currently available - *Dance Craze*, The Special A.K.A.'s *On Film*, and one called *Specials* which is really just the band's early promo videos, together with bits from *On Film*. Again there are countless bootleg videos showing 2 Tone bands on TV programmes that you come across now and then.

Since the first edition of this book, Chrysalis have released a Specials' album entitled *Singles* which offered nothing new to the true fan, unless you had worn out the original singles. Still, at least it put the band back in the charts with a high of number nine.

The only other book on 2 Tone is the *Two Tone Book For Rude Boys*, long since deleted by Omnibus Press. It's a bit confusing in both content and layout, but is well worth picking up if you come across it.

A magazine called *Ska '80* made an appearance way back when, and featured the 2 Tone bands and associated ones like Dexy's Midnight Runners. It was just a one-off, as were the two magazines published to coincide with the release of the film *Dance Craze*. *The History Of Rock* series dedicated an issue to 2 Tone too.

The above is still not exhaustive and I would welcome any additions and corrections should we publish a further edition of this book.

ALSO FROM S.T. PUBLISHING

Total Madness by George Marshall
120 page book with colour and black and white photos charting the rise and fall of Camden Town's favourite sons, Madness. It takes you from the days when the band were still known as The Invaders, right through to the decision to reform in 1992. Includes full discography. £9.95

Bad Manners by George Marshall
52 page booklet with black and white photos telling the story of Bad Manners, the band who hit the charts with classics like *Lorraine*, *Lip Up Fatty*, *Special Brew* and lots more. A must for Manners fans. Limited edition of 1,000 printed. £3.50

Watching The Rich Kids by Arthur Kay
104 page book with photos destined to become a street classic. Arthur Kay takes you on a tour of the backstreets of rock n' roll which he knows only too well. Includes material on cult ska favourites, The Originals, and the Oi!some Last Resort. £5.95

Spirit Of '69 - A Skinhead Bible by George Marshall
168 page book packed with photos and cuttings. This book gives the first detailed account of the skinhead cult from the late Sixties to the present day, with chapters on skinhead reggae, 2 Tone, Oi!, today's scene, fashion and lots more. Welcome to the land of the bovver brigade! £8.95

The Complete Richard Allen Volume One
Now back in print, the Richard Allen novels that charted youth cults throughout the 1970s. **Volume One** contains three great novels, **Skinhead, Suedehead** and **Skinhead Escapes**. £6.95

The Complete Richard Allen Volume Two
Three more classics from the king of youth cult fiction. **Volume Two** contains **Skinhead Girls, Sorts** and **Knuckle Girls**. £6.95

All of the above books are available direct from the publishers. We send all books post free in the U.K., but ask overseas readers to write first before ordering. If you would like full details of our titles and a free copy of **Skinhead Times** just send a large SSAE (U.K. only) or 2 IRCs (overseas and available from post offices) to S.T. Publishing, P.O. Box 12, Dunoon, Argyll. PA23 7BQ. Scotland.